Making More Money Retailing

Low-Cost Ideas For Successful Merchandising And Boosting Profits From Your Retail Store

Barbara Lambesis & Susan Ratliff

Marketing Methods Press
Phoenix, Arizona

Library of Congress Catalog Card Number: 94-075853

ISBN 0-9624798-8-8

Authors, Barbara Lambesis & Susan Ratliff

Printed in the United States of America

Quantity discounts are available from the publisher.

Dedication

To the talented retail store owners and merchants who make shopping a wonderful, enjoyable experience. May your cash registers ring continuously.

Table Of Contents

Introduction 1

Chapter 1 - Making Money As A Retail Store Owner 5
Examine Your Motives * Do Your Market Research * Develop The Right
Approach * Enhance The Retail Concept With Environment * Stick To Your
Niche * Remember, It's A Business

Chapter 2 - Stores That Make Money 11
Customer Traffic Is Essential * Location, Location, Location * Convenience
* Operating Days And Hours * Competing For Customers

Chapter 3 - Customer Service 19
The Customer Is King * Staffing The Store * Hire Attitude * Set Standards
* Communicate The Standards * Reward Performance * Convenience *
Customer Etiquette

Chapter 4 - Creating Excitement 29
Temporary Displays * Basic Display Structures * Professional Display
Companies * Tents And Awnings * Professional Signs * Product
Presentation Demonstrations * Theme Merchandise And Holiday
Packaging * Use Color Consistently * Lighting * Keep It Clean And Neat

Chapter 5 - Sharpen Your Sales Skills 47
Set Goals For Sales * Project A Professional Image * Clothes That Make The
Sale * A Professional Attitude * Using Body Language To Your Advantage
* Your Sales Presentation * Product Knowledge Is Essential * Why People
Buy * Overcoming Objections * Add-On Selling

Chapter 6 - Ideas For Making More Money 63
Exhibit Marketing At Weekend Events * Carts And Kiosks * Mail Order *
Personal Shopper * Telephone Sales

Chapter 7 - Low-cost Promotion For Your Retail Store . . .75
Use Multiple Methods And Be Consistent * Advertising * Personal Sales *
Packaging * Public Relations And Publicity * Sales Incentives * Get
Organized * Stick To Your Plan * Give It Time To Work

Chapter 8 - Changing Direction 131
When Things Are Not Working * Assessing The Market * Looking At
Options * Making A Business Decision.

INTRODUCTION

Inspiration and motivation are essential for success--especially when it comes to launching and operating a retail business. Being inspired and motivated, however, isn't enough. Today, you also must have knowledge to succeed. That's why learning basic business principles is absolutely necessary for anyone whose goals include becoming a successful owner of a retail business. Being a successful retail entrepreneur means using inspiration, motivation and knowledge to reach your goals.

Knowledge is power, and the power to gain the methods to achieve financial independence through retail marketing is outlined in this book. Many of the instructions, techniques and skills necessary to build a successful, profitable enterprise are explained. Whether you're a beginner or a seasoned veteran at retail merchandising, the information contained in this handbook will help you make more money selling products at your store.

What makes a small retail shop appealing? Usually it's the personal, friendly, hands-on attention given to it by its owner. Because the owner is involved in all aspects of the business, the store can respond quickly to customers and their needs. That's a competitive advantage large chain stores don't enjoy.

Eleanor Roosevelt once said, "The future belongs to those who believe in the beauty of their dreams." Many people talk about their goals and dreams, but few actually attempt to fulfill them. If your dream is to develop a profitable retail business, this book provides the motivation and much of the "know how" you will need to lessen the risks involved in business ownership.

While building a retail business, every owner will confront many challenges, as well as realize many rewards. Making money may be the primary reason for starting a retail business, but other benefits and incentives also can be derived from the experience. Many believe the personal satisfaction they gain from controlling the workplace, improving business acumen, interacting with people, and receiving admiration and respect from peers is worth as much as money.

Speaking of money, this book is not about bookkeeping or the financial analysis and management necessary to run a profitable store. Those areas are critically important to success and could be the subject of an entire book. This book is about marketing, merchandising and promoting your store so you can make more money by making more sales.

The authors of this book bring years of experience and know-how to the reader. Both are successful business women and both have shared their ideas and methods as speakers and seminar presenters throughout the United States and Canada. Each is a small business advocate.

In 1989, Susan Ratliff was honored as Arizona's Entrepreneurial Mother of the Year, by the Entrepreneurial

Mothers Association. In 1992, she was named Small Business Owner of the Year by the Scottsdale Arizona Chamber of Commerce.

Barbara Lambesis has received numerous local and national awards for her professional endeavors and has held top leadership positions in several professional associations. Most recently she was named Woman Business Advocate of the Year by the Phoenix Chapter of the National Association of Women Business Owners.

The public recognition and exposure generated by these awards have increased the personal self-confidence and business credibility of both authors, not to mention their success as entrepreneurs.

Most people who succeed do so because they love what they do. The authors are happy to share their successful experiences and knowledge with organizations and groups who wish to sponsor their informative workshops and seminars on how to become successful at retail marketing utilizing the profitable techniques outlined in this book.

For information, write to the address below.

Marketing Methods Press
1413 E. Marshall Avenue
Phoenix, Arizona 85014

CHAPTER ONE

Making Money As A Retail Store Owner

If you have experience as a retail store owner, this chapter will refresh your memory about some simple, but important, principles that cannot be overlooked if you want your store to make money. If you have never owned and operated a retail establishment in the past, read this chapter carefully! It should help you avoid the mistakes that often lead to disaster for first time retail operators.

Examine Your Motives

This sounds elementary and maybe even patronizing, but it's really important for owners to be very clear about their motivations for investing their money, time and ego in a store. While a few owners have been able to parlay their special interests and lifestyle preferences into a retail store that allows them to surround themselves with products and people who share a passionate interest in an special area, most cannot. Just consider the following examples of misguided motivations.

One woman opened a flower shop because she just loved flowers. She assumed her enthusiasm for flowers would be enough to make her flower shop a success. She had no experience in the business. None! She had nothing unique to offer customers in an already saturated marketplace. Moreover, she had no idea how to control her perishable inventory. After dumping her life savings into a flower shop, she had to close down the enterprise within six months. She could have saved herself time, money and heartbreak by simply expanding her garden or taking trips to national flower shows.

Another woman loved to make craft items. After her children had grown, she decided to open a small craft supply store. Her reasoning was simple. She thought she could create her own craft studio and wait on customers as she crafted. Having a store also meant she could get her personal supplies wholesale. She thought owning a store would be a vehicle to expand her hobby. Unfortunately, serving customers was an annoyance, so it didn't take the customers long to figure out they could spend their money elsewhere in a store that would appreciate their business. The idea that a store could be a money-making vehicle for expanding a hobby was a failure and the shop soon closed.

A laid-off engineer from a electronics company was crazy about Southwest Indian cultures. Over the years he had visited the the reservations, purchased numerous artifacts, and absorbed everything he could about the history and cultural heritage of many tribes. The Navajo nation was of special interest. He thought everyone would be interested in dining at a restaurant with authentic Navajo cuisine. After dumping his severance pay into remodeling a very large, abandoned family-style restaurant once belonging to a chain, he hired local Navajos and opened the doors. Standing by the door in his velvet, Navajo-style shirt and silver jewelry he was ready to start a new career combining his life-long interest with a business.

Unfortunately, this new restaurateur was in for a very expensive shock. The reason the urban, sophisticated Southwest city never had a restaurant with Navajo cuisine before was simple. Not many people were interested in eating high-priced, bland mutton stew with blue corn bread in a establishment without a liquor license. Not many people found Navajo mannerisms, such as the custom which considers it rude to look someone directly in the eye and a natural shyness that makes smiles a rarity, the type of attributes that make for a friendly, welcoming hostess and serving staff.

His enthusiasm for the Navajo culture and his heartfelt desire to create jobs for urban Navajo people had blinded his business reasoning. His lack of restaurant experience was evident by leasing an inappropriate facility and not realizing that profit margins are highest from bar sales from which few food establishments can survive without. In addition, he failed to do even the simplest of market research to determine in advance if his restaurant idea could be a success. The restaurant didn't last six weeks.

The point of these stories is the same. If you want your retail store to make money, it must be run as a business. For the owner to make the best business decisions, those that will favorably impact the bottom line, the primary motivation for operating any retail store must be strictly a business, dollar and cents one. Before you open a store or continue to struggle operating an existing one, examine again your motivations.

Remember, it's a business! If you really haven't the personality of a dedicated, entrepreneurial, bottom-line, customer-loving business owner, there are many easier and less risky ways to make a living.

Do Your Market Research

Money-making retail establishments have savvy owners. These are owners who take the time to study the marketplace before they open a store. Usually they are able to find a special need in the market and fill it with a store offering products that develop a new or exciting retailing concept.

Do your homework. Carefully review the demographics of an area to learn as much as you can about the people living there. Determine age, sex, ethnic background, education, buying habits, and income of potential customers. Then, size up the retail scene. Develop a list of all the types of stores vying for customers in the market territory you are considering. Look for opportunities. Identify unmet needs. Find unsatisfied buyers looking for a new and different shopping experience. Simply put, find a need and fill it. Give the customers what they want, not necessarily what you like or products for which you are personally partial.

Retailing everywhere will be competitive. However, you can improve your chances for success if you target your market carefully and offer a shopping experience that is unique and different, even if the products are common and familiar. Determine in advance if enough potential customers live and work in your territory for a store to make money from your retail concept.

Develop The Right Approach

Finding products to sell is not the problem. Developing the right retailing concept is the challenge. The most successful, money-making, independent retail stores in recent years have been niche retailers or specialty retailers. Many of these stores are small in space, but high in profit making.

These stores specialize in one type of product, providing a greater variety and selection then can be found in most stores. Some carry items around a theme.

For example, one successful retail store carries only rare papers, specializing in handmade paper and speciality papers from around the world. Another store offers everything for wild birds - feeders, houses, baths, seed, bird books, binoculars, and other bird watching items.

Decide whether you will offer items that are old and familiar or new and different. This decision will be made by understanding your potential customer's buying habits. Are consumers in your territory attracted to the new and unique or are they more comfortable purchasing old standby products? If people in your territory are not innovators and are not excited by trying the latest things, you will do best to stick with products that require little risk to purchase.

Enhance The Retailing Concept With Environment

Merchandise will move out the door faster when presented in the right atmosphere. The environment in which you offer your products should help put the customer in the mood to buy and should directly enhance the retailing concept being developed.

For example, in the case of the store offering bird watching items, the interior was designed to resemble the edge of a forest and part of a backyard. Shoppers instantly could imagine themselves using the offered items to observe wild birds in their yards or on a hike in the forest. The staff wore khaki shorts and t-shirts imprinted with bird heat transfers. Bird calls were softly piped over the speaker system. Shoppers loved to visit the store and many otherwise not interested people became bird watchers and customers as a result of their visit. Because the merchandise was offered in a environment that reinforced the theme of the products, customers found the shopping experience exciting, educational and fun.

Stick To Your Niche

Once you have found the right retailing concept for your market, stick to it for as long as possible. Develop, enhance and improve your niche or speciality store as you ride the wave of success, but don't mess with the basic concept. By trying to diversify and be all things to all people, an independent retail store will lose the one advantage it can have over the larger retailers - its uniqueness and staff expertise in a special product area.

Remember, It's A Business

Yes, the store owner should benefit in many ways beyond the income produced by the enterprise. Ideally a store owner should love the products, enjoy the company of customers and staff, take pride in building a business and receive satisfaction from creating an interesting store. Even so, the owner must never loose sight of the fact the store is a business, and as a business it cannot survive if the owner doesn't take a serious business-like approach to operating it. Always remember, it's more than a store, it's a business.

CHAPTER TWO

Stores That Make Money

There are hundreds of retail stores for shoppers to choose from each time they go out to make a purchase. Not every store is successful. Some stores make more money than others, while some stores don't make enough money to stay open very long. Therefore, it is essential to PLAN how to structure your retail business and how to design your store so it will generate the most profit from the sale of your particular merchandise. Good planning is the key to success and it will maximize your store's potential for long-term survival.

To be a successful retail store owner, you must concentrate initial efforts on learning everything you can about retailing and about how to develop a successful business strategy. Pay attention to the details that will keep you from making costly mistakes and will put you on the road to success and profits quickly. If you have been in business for some period and the store just isn't doing as well as you would like, now is the time to reassess your entire approach to retailing.

Customer Traffic Is Essential

The first and most important element necessary for successful retailing is customer traffic. Selling success is tied directly to how many people walk into your store. Selling is a numbers game. The higher the number of people in your store, especially those who are qualified shoppers, the greater the potential for sales and profit. Unless enough buyers consistently enter your establishment, none of your other sales and marketing efforts will matter. So, always look first at the factors that will expose your merchandise to the largest number of potential, qualified buyers at the lowest possible cost. This should be your primary consideration when developing or assessing your retailing strategy.

Location, Location, Location

Location is everything in retailing, because the right location is absolutely essential to success. Site selection is easier when you know the characteristics of your typical customer and the market you plan to serve. Very early in your planning, determine who is most likely to buy what you intend to sell, who wants or needs what you have to offer. These people are your potential customers, your specific type of buyer. Determine if they are likely to be mothers, grandparents, business managers, store owners, retirees, men, women or teenagers. Determine their household income and what level of education they are likely to have achieved. The more you know about your typical customers, the easier it will be to find the right location.

For example, the potential customer of a retailer who sells baby items will be most likely a female parent, a female grandparent or a relative or friend of the mother. Office products are purchased by business owners and office managers. Custom leather briefcases will attract buyers with an executive business background. Gift items appeal to a wider audience, but are purchased most often by women.

Understanding your customer will help you achieve purposeful marketing and will maximize your selling efforts. The chances of making a sale increase substantially when seven out of ten people coming to your retail setting might need or want what you have to offer. Retailers who choose to ignore the importance of pinpointing their potential customers can waste substantial time and money without generating enough sales to make the business successful. So, analyze the characteristics of the customer most likely to purchase your merchandise. Then, find out if the locations you are considering will cater to these people. Do this before you sign a lease.

Convenience

Depending on the price of your products, your location must be convenient to the customers who can afford to buy what you plan to sell. In other words, if your products and prices are upscale, your location must be convenient to upscale customers; that is, close to where they live or work. Today's customers live in a busy, fast-paced society. All things being equal, a customer will make a purchase at the most convenient location. So, determine how far a customer must travel to get to the locations you are considering and give the edge to those with the shortest distance.

Traffic patterns and parking also are part of the convenience factor. The first factor to consider is parking. There must be adequate and convenient parking available near the location to encourage lots of customers to visit your store. Nothing is more discouraging to a potential shopper than driving around for ten minutes looking for a place to park, then walking blocks to the entrance. If customers start thinking about carrying purchases several blocks and having to remember where they parked, there's a good chance they will not stop. If close-by parking is free and unrestricted and the parking lot is easy to maneuver, your location has a definite advantage. On the other hand, if street parking is metered and difficult to find or a parking garage with excessive charges is narrow and difficult to negotiate, customer traffic will be much more difficult to build.

The second factor is exposure. A great location must have good exposure. Determine if the store will have direct exposure to a major street. When people drive by and are able to see the establishment, many will be curious and will stop to see what's being offered. Excellent visibility from the street can double walk-in traffic and name recognition. Smart shop owners will make sure there are large, eye-catching signs identifying the store and may even rent billboards at nearby intersections announcing its presence and directing people to their store.

The side of the street on which your store is located also makes a big difference. Stores located on the side of the street in which traffic is "going home" always do better than stores on the side of the street on which traffic is "going to work." Also, if your store will depend heavily on female customers, remember most women drivers try to avoid making left hand turns across two lanes of traffic and also hesitate to slow down to make a turn on a heavily travelled roadway with speeding traffic.

When considering a location, be sure to check the vehicle access to determine if the entry ways and exists onto the traffic lane are wide and easy to negotiate. If you are planning a store in an urban area, also check on access to public transportation, which is always important to seniors, handicapped individuals and children.

No matter how wonderful your products, how enticing your prices and how much you advertise, if your location is not convenient in every way to your customers, your retail store will never reach its potential and could be doomed to failure.

Most communities zone special areas for commercial or trade use. Stores are found in groups in these areas. Regional or mega shopping malls, local shopping malls, neighborhood strip shopping centers in the suburbs, main street business districts in small towns, and highway off-ramp commercial centers compose the most typical retail site locations. The main difference between each alternative boils down to foot-traffic and rental rates. The higher the foot traffic the higher the rental rate.

So, when assessing the location of your retail operation, select the one that is most convenient to your customers and has the highest amount of foot traffic for the rental rate you can afford.

Operating Days And Hours

Before signing a lease, find out how many selling days per week and what restrictions on hours of operation are attached to a rental agreement. Most owners who rent in small retail centers usually are allowed to set their own business hours. However, shopping malls and some landlords have restrictions on the hours the store can or must be open to the public.

Operational hours also will have an impact on your success as a retailer. For example, if products are aimed at employed people, make sure the store can be open early and close late so customers can drop by before or after work, in addition to being open both Saturday and Sunday for weekend only shoppers.

Competing For Customers

Do not be afraid of competition! Competition is healthy. When competitors have retail outlets near a site you are considering, it usually confirms that the products you intend to sell will appeal to the customers in the area. When you find other stores with products similar to yours, use the opportunity to learn from them and analyze their strengths and weaknesses. Compare your offerings with that of the competition for design, quality and special services like delivery, shipping or gift wrapping. Keep abreast of exactly what the competition is selling; then give the public something a bit different.

For years, auto dealers have located in the same general area. They found that a customer interested in buying a car doesn't want to drive all over town to see different makes and models. All dealers profit by getting shoppers to their general area. If the customer doesn't find what he's looking for at one dealership, he can cross the street to continue the search. That approach also may work for gifts, apparel, sporting goods, antiques and consignment items.

For example, consider decorated T-shirts. Many different merchants sell T-shirts at stores in any given shopping district. If you look carefully at each merchant's product, you'll notice that some sell screen printed shirts, some sell spin art T-shirts, some sell hand-painted designs, some offer appliqued styles and some sell T-shirts decorated with ribbon. The point is, each merchant has found a different way to sell the same basic product, thus offering a variety of choices to appeal to differing customer tastes.

Do not be discouraged from renting space at a location that has direct competition. First, check the demographics to determine how many potential customers the store can attract, then offer something different or give your customers products with a new twist. If you still cringe at the thought of having direct competition at the same location, think about this: How many times have you driven down the street and passed by a McDonald's fast food restaurant on one corner and Burger King directly across the street? Each sells very similar products, at almost identical prices, in similar surroundings. So, why should these two corporate giants locate so close to one another? First, because market research probably showed there was plenty of business for both. Second, each one feeds off the aggressive advertising and promotional efforts of the other. And finally, they are marketing to a similar audience. Anyone driving by, in the mood for a burger, will pull into one restaurant or the other, depending on brand loyalty or convenience of access. The point is, in the right location, there usually is plenty of business for everyone.

On the other hand, if you find an area where your potential customers are not being served by stores offering products similar to yours and the demographics indicate enough potential customers are available to sustain a store, you may be able to fill a void in marketplace. You'll have the opportunity to capture that particular market, competition free.

CHAPTER THREE

Customer Service

There are really only two advantages independent retail shops can have over large category killers and discount chains. The first is unique merchandise. By offering items that cannot be found in mass market stores, an independent retailer can carve out a special niche and attract customers who are looking for the unusual and unique in the items they purchase. The other advantage, if delivered, is quality customer service. Frankly, of the two advantages available to the independents, customer service is the most important.

The Customer Is King

Remember, it is unlikely an independent store will ever be able to beat a larger competitor's price. Therefore, a store owner must give his customers something more - something worth the extra cost. It sounds trite, but the customer should always be made to feel that he or she is the most important person alive. Because few of us experience that feeling when we are shopping, it is always a surprise and shock when we are the recipient of great customer service. It also gets our attention. Moreover, extraordinary customer service is the single most important element required to develop a loyal customer base.

Everyone talks about customer service but few deliver it. Why? Because most people define customer service differently. In addition, we tend to assume that when we talk in general terms about giving customers good service, all store employees automatically should know what that means.

If a store can increase its competitive advantage by providing top-notch customer service, there are a number of things every store owner should consider.

Staffing The Store

No one can be as enthusiastic about the merchandise and the store as the owner. Therefore, the owner should stay on the selling floor and do the selling personally, whenever possible. Sales increase when a customer can ask questions concerning the merchandise and get knowledgeable answers from friendly sales staff. Sales also increase when customers feel the owner is taking a personal interest in the customer's shopping experience. Getting out of your office and on to the store floor is essential if you want to meet and greet shoppers and if you want to stay in touch with your customer's needs and wants. When you cannot be present, always leave the sales floor in the hands of someone who will take the same pride in serving customers as you do.

Because you cannot do everything by yourself, store owners are forced to hire employees to assist with running the enterprise. If customer service is a key to success, your hiring practices will significantly impact your store's financial and long-term success. Therefore, when staffing your store, look beyond skills and experience when hiring new employees.

Hire Attitude

Every employee of your store who will come in contact with customers MUST have a people pleasing personality. Period. Therefore, hire attitude. You can always train people to run the register, stock the shelves and tag the merchandise. You cannot, however, train someone to change their basic personality type. If job applicants do not smile throughout the job interview, it is very unlikely they will smile throughout their work shifts.

Good customer service starts with individuals who genuinely like people, who are interested in satisfying customer needs and who are willing to make the customer's shopping experience a pleasant one. These employees also will go the extra mile to make a customer happy.

If you have employees who are not good with customers, move them to jobs that do not require customer contact or replace them. That goes for relatives, too. A shop owner cannot afford to have customers come in contact with insensitive personnel. These are individuals who radiate negative vibrations at worst or are simply ambivalent at best. If it means you must fire your spouse, child or nephew to improve customer service, do it.

Set Standards

Don't assume that all employees understand what you, the business owner, mean by quality customer service. Spell it out exactly by setting measurable standards. For example, you may wish to set standards for the way in which customers are greeted when they enter the store. Or, the manner in which the store will accept returns. Or, how quickly and in which manner the telephones are answered. Or, the extent to which the store will attempt to get or modify an item for a customer.

Or, the freedom with which the sales staff will assist a customer in solving a problem or request. Determine what you believe constitutes superior customer service in your retail category. Then, set measurable standards and monitor its delivery.

Communicate The Standards

Once you have defined customer service for your store, communicate it over and over to the staff. First, write it down and make copies to give to all employees. Post the standards on the bulletin board. Review the standards with employees on a regular basis - as often as once a week at a brief employee staff meeting. Counsel with each employee individually when you notice a problem in meeting any standard. Remind employees, and yourself, that staff performance will be evaluated on how well an employee provides customer service according to the standards set for the business.

Reward Performance

Reward and recognition are the best ways to reinforce the importance of high standards of customer service and the goals all staff members are working to achieve. Don't wait for the annual employee review to recognize employees that best serve customers. Delivering rewards little and often is a far better method for reinforcing desired behavior.

Provide verbal recognition frequently. For example, "That was a great job you did with Mrs. Jones, Kathy. Your efforts made her one happy customer. Thanks!" The point is, tell your employees that they are doing the right thing when you see them providing good service. Do it in front of the other staff members so they, too, can get the idea.

Pass out little rewards for small efforts and bigger rewards for superior efforts. For example, one store owner frequently passes out candy bars to employees who are trying hard to deliver exceptional service with a note that says, "Thanks for doing the best you can to make our customers happy." Another store owner gives out $25 bonus checks to employees who have done a superior job in dealing with a difficult customer service problem.

Customers like to feel appreciated, but so do employees. If you want your employees to understand and cooperate with your customer service program, you must reinforce its importance by acknowledging and rewarding employee's efforts to meet your store's standards.

Convenience

Today's shoppers are pressed for time. So, convenience plays a huge role in most purchasing decisions. Consider for a moment an experience most shoppers have encountered. Upon entering a store, the shopper has difficulty finding what he's looking for and is unable to locate a sales assistant to help. Finally, after locating the desired items the shopper gets to the check-out line only to find it backed up ten deep. Pressed for time and annoyed by his experience, the shopper drops the merchandise and walks out of the store without making a purchase.

Once you have located your store in the most convenient location, and done all you can to make access and parking easy, do an internal "convenience audit." When a shopper enters the store, how easy it is for the shopper to make a purchase? Remember, successful stores make is as easy and painless to buy the store's merchandise. The most successful stores make it an enjoyable experience.

Ask yourself these questions:

*   Is the store arranged so shoppers can find merchandise easily?

*   Do signs direct shoppers to merchandise categories?

*   Is the merchandise marked and are prices easy to read?

*   Can customers get their questions asked promptly and courteously?

*   Is there a place for customers to inspect or try on/out merchandise?

*   Can the sales transaction be done quickly and efficiently?

*   Does the cashier always have adequate change and does the store accept checks and credit cards?

Have someone shop your store and report back the details of the experience. Then, identify the problem areas and ask employees to help you develop better ways of operating the store to give superior, convenient customer service.

Customer Etiquette

Yes, there are general rules of etiquette that govern the actions of store owners who respect their customers, and it's wise to practice them. Experienced, successful shop owners are aware of these courtesies, but many new owners are not familiar with them. The common sense rules that follow will keep the customers happy and will contribute to making the experience of running your store pleasant and successful, too.

Don't Smoke

Even if smoking is permitted by local laws, don't do it in the store or in the store's backrooms. Smoking will alienate employees and customers. If you or your employees must smoke, go outside to a designated smoking area away from the shop. Never stand in the front doorway to have a smoke.

Don't Tie Up Customers With Idle Conversation

Sharing ideas and making friends with customers is part of the fun associated with operating a store. Just remember, though, customers came to the establishment to make a purchase and that is their first priority. Be considerate of their time, since many may be in a hurry.

Don't Tie Up Other Sales Staff With Idle Conversation

It's simple; the sales staff cannot acknowledge and help shoppers if they are engaged in a discussion with the owner or another member of the sales staff. Customers often are reluctant to interrupt with questions when a sales person is talking to someone.

Again, the workplace is a social outlet for employees; and, staffers should be encouraged to get along. Nevertheless, they must be alert during occasional conversations with each other and always immediately direct themselves to shoppers who enter the store. In addition, employees should never bother the sales staff when they are busy with customers.

Don't Develop A Negative Attitude

Nothing is more annoying than an employee or owner who moans, groans and complains about everything. Even when sales are poor, it is useless to dwell on it. Rather than grumble about slow sales, use the time to make notes on possible reasons why traffic is poor or why your merchandise is not selling. Rearrange the merchandise, go over sales skills with the staff, and evaluate your store's image and promotional methods. No matter how unhappy you are, keep your complaints to yourself.

Don't Eat In View Of The Customers

Leave the sales floor when you wish to eat. If you are working the store by yourself, it may be impossible to get away for a lunch break. If you must eat on the floor, do so as inconspicuously as possible.

Don't "Badmouth" The Competition

Mothers have said for years, "If you don't have something nice to say, don't say anything." Every shop owner should heed those words. Believe it or not, some owners think the only way they can make a sale is to verbally rundown their competition. This type of behavior is improper and unprofessional.

Today's consumers are sophisticated. They rarely are swayed by negative comments, and often resent the shopkeeper who makes them. Never "badmouth" the competition in an attempt to make your store look better. You'll do best if you sell your products on their own merits.

Don't Leave Your Store Unoccupied For Long Periods

Sometimes, in an emergency, it may be is necessary to leave your store unattended, especially when you are working the store alone. Try to avoid leaving the premises for extended periods. If you must leave, place a sign for everyone to see indicating when you will be back. That way, if customers need to see you, they will know when to return to your shop. A better solution is to find someone who will cover the store and keep it open in your absence.

Don't Make Excessive Noise

When the volume is too high on the background music or on video equipment used in a product presentation, customers will not be able to converse easily with the sales staff. Offensive noise also can come from salespeople who talk too loud. Make sure the sound of your sales presentation stays within the confines of your space and always keep background music low.

Don't Bring Children Or Pets To The Store

This may seem obvious, but occasionally we find shops where children of owners run around the store, handling merchandise and making a general nuisance of themselves. When young children run wild throughout the store, it's disturbing and inappropriate. Pets also do not belong at your store; unless, of course, you own a pet shop.

CHAPTER FOUR

Creating Excitement

Stop and Look!! That's what effective store fronts, window designs and sales aids say to passing shoppers. Retailers must fight for the shopper's attention, so the most attractive, unusual or eye-catching merchandise displays or store windows are the ones that get noticed. With this in mind, don't take the design of your store front, floor space and store fixtures, as well as the display of your products for granted.

Merchandising is everything you do to attract shoppers and get them to buy your products. So, pay careful attention to such details as the accent colors of a temporary display, the methods employed to present products, the materials utilized to construct the display shelves and racks and the signs that identify your business and products.

The entire selling environment should reflect the right image and attract customers most likely to purchase your offerings. Whenever possible, employ an interior designer with retail store experience to help you attain a coordinated look and feel to your store. Determine what image the store will have - conservative, feminine, high tech, country. Then, make sure the colors, wall coverings, fixtures, carpet, sales counters and lighting all fit the image and are consistent with your overall theme and approach. Owners who make the most of their floor space make the most money.

Temporary Displays

Use temporary displays to showcase merchandise and keep the store fresh and interesting. Deciding which products to display can be challenging. Feature new products, feature hot products, or feature products that fit a theme and can be pulled from various parts of the store. To gain the most attention and draw shoppers into the store, place displays in the window, near the front of the store or in a highly visible, high traffic area.

The first step necessary to create an effective merchandise display is to design the type of structure that will best present the products or services. Then, select the materials to construct it. Create a temporary display structure that has some flexibility. That way you can modify the structure and use it over and over.

There are many designs to consider when planning temporary displays and changing in-store merchandise exhibits. The simplest way to determine which type is best is to study the displays at stores in shopping malls and trade shows. Your temporary display will impact your image and either enhance or detract from the appeal of the products. Therefore, take special care in planning and creating temporary merchandise displays.

When planning a display, determine how the products are best viewed by the buyer. Should they be displayed at eye level, suspended from above, placed on shelves, hung on a wall, or laid on the floor? Next, consider your display theme, if any, and what props will enhance the presentation of the merchandise. Then, give some thought to the ease of assembly, time required for set-up and break-down, weight of the materials, and repeat use and storage requirements.

Many merchants just starting their businesses have limited funds with which to develop displays. Lots of creativity, imagination and resourcefulness, however, can make up for lack of money. This chapter will provide many ideas for low-cost construction materials and items you can use to create attractive and effective displays to showcase your merchandise or services.

Basic Display Structures

Tables

The most commonly used display structure is the lightweight, folding table. Aluminum tables are inexpensive and can be found at most do-it-yourself building supply stores. Tables are available in 5, 6, or 8 foot lengths, and usually are 2 or 2 1/2 feet wide. Six-foot tables are the most popular, since they allow for a wide variety of configurations.

Tables also can be made by simply laying a piece of plywood, in any desired size, over two saw horses. When

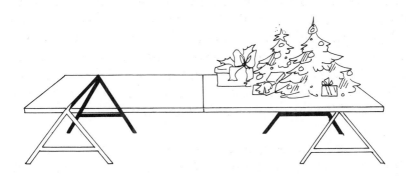

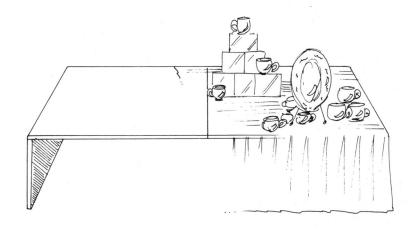

draped with a cloth, these make-shift tables look fine. Tables also can be made by cutting a hollow door in half, hinging it back together and laying it over metal legs.

Small round tables with removable legs also are available at low cost from home improvement stores and mass market retailers. In addition, colorful, floor-length table coverings usually are available to fit the tables.

Table Coverings

Draping for your display tables is important to the presentation of the merchandise and should complement your products, display and store decor. All sides of your tables that are exposed to the public should be covered to within a few inches from the floor. The easiest way to cover a table is to drape it with a rectangular piece of cloth that covers all sides. Always gather the excess cloth at the corners and pin it back so no one will trip over the cover. Placing another cloth of a contrasting color or a deeper hue over the top of the table can make the display table more attractive.

As your business grows, invest some of your profits to improve your display tables. While a pinned-back cloth is cheap and easy, the serious retailer eventually will invest in more sophisticated table coverings. Want to put more pizzazz in your table display? Find ways to incorporate some unusual materials into the presentation of your products. Retailers

have created attractive table covers using quilts, grass cloth, straw mats, cork board and beach towels. Others have added marbles, tissue paper, cotton balls, rhinestones, sand, confetti and other items to create interest and accent their products.

Shelves

Temporary shelves offer versatility in the display area, but they must be easy to assemble and store to be practical. One of the most popular ways to make shelves for a portable

display is to use a wooden, three-panel screen as a base and use 1-foot by 6-foot boards as shelves. Another shelf display can be made by attractively painting two,

6-foot step ladders and placing boards or wooden dowels across each rung of the ladder.

Panels

Panels form the basis of many interesting and effective displays. Many are lightweight and easy for one person to handle. Panels are versatile and can be used in a variety of

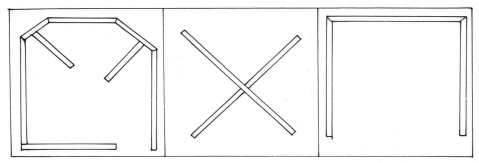

configurations. In addition, many low- cost materials such as pegboard, lattice, metal grids and grooved wallboard can be used to construct temporary or permanent display panels.

Pegboard

Framed artwork, calligraphy or photography need a backdrop to be displayed effectively. Pegboard is an excellent display material, since it is very versatile and inexpensive. An "X" frame or "A" frame display can be fashioned from pegboard. These display styles are easy to erect and move around the floor. Another option is to construct a triangular display of pegboard. This style allows three sides for displaying products. Pegboard can be attached directly to a wall, as well.

Another alternative is to mount sheets of pegboard on wooden or metal legs. A variety of metal hooks, plexiglass

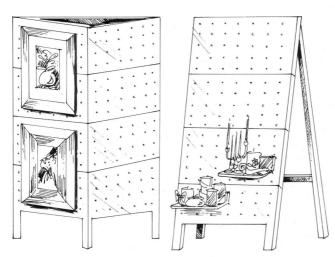

display pieces and shelf fixtures are made specif- ically for use with pegboard. You can find these items at outlets that sell store display fixtures. Look in the Yellow Pages under "Display."

Lattice

An inexpensive, but attractive material to use in a display is wooden lattice. Found at most building supply stores, lattice usually is available in 4-foot by 8-foot sheets. Don't buy flimsy lattice used for garden plants and flowers. Use lattice with thick diagonal slats.

This material is excellent for displaying items that should be hung, such as clothing or dried flower arrangements. Hang lattice in the same manner as pegboard. Lattice panels also can be mounted on legs, made into folding screens or attached to walls.

Wire Grid Panels

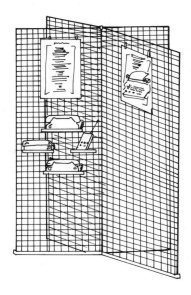

Wire grid panels can be assembled in a variety of ways and can easily be expanded to fit your changing needs. Many accessories and display attachments such as baskets, shelves, hooks, railings and trays can be purchased for use with wire grids. Wire grids can create a very professional, attractive and durable display for merchandise. They are, however, expensive and heavy to erect.

Modular Wire Cubes

Modular wire cubes are popular and are an inexpensive alternative to heavy, metal wire grids. Small and easy to assemble, the cubes are made of lightweight, plastic-coated wire panels that snap together with plastic connectors. Assemble an entire wall of cubes or a small custom unit to display shirts, gift items, sporting goods or any stackable merchandise. Mini grids come in several colors and utilize the same accessories as heavy wire grids.

Slatwall Panels

Slatwall panels, also known as grooved wallboard, is a multi-purpose display material. Although heavy, grooved slatboard comes in 4-foot by 8- foot sheets which can be cut to any size. The grooves separating each slat of wood are

designed to hold display fixtures such as hooks, baskets, and shelves. The panels come ready to paint, laminated in colored finishes, or finished in a variety of wood veneers.

Professional Display Companies

Many display companies have manufacturing capabilities and can customize a display to your exact specifications. They can build anything, from a simple backdrop to a vendor cart similar to those seen in shopping malls. You may wish to consider these options after you have some experience and are ready to upgrade your interior with more permanent displays.

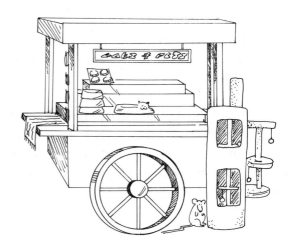

Tents And Awnings

Tents and awnings come in many configurations and materials and can be used successfully inside a retail store to create eye-catching display areas. Most use an aluminum or PVC pipe frame, with a canvas or vinyl covering that fits over the assembly. Vendors that make and sell them for a reasonable fee usually can be found at flea markets or swap meets. Awning companies also stock a variety of tents and awnings suitable for exhibits and will rent them, as well.

Professional Signs

Signs that identify your business or communicate sales messages to shoppers are an important part of a merchant's display. Many sign companies are able to produce colorful, professionally lettered signs or banners the same day you order them. Give careful thought to the colors, style of the lettering and size of your inside signs and coordinate these elements with those of your decor and sales literature whenever possible. A logo or company symbol on your sign helps to reinforce your identity to the public.

The size of the sign and the lettering will determine how easy it is to read. Keep in mind 3-inch lettering can be read from 70 to 80 feet and 1-inch lettering from 10 to 30 feet. Avoid hand lettering any signs yourself, unless you are a graphic artist.

Your outside store sign also is critical to your success. Hire a sign company and give your store a professional image with professional looking signs. Remember the old saying, a business with no sign, is a sign of no business.

Product Presentation

Elevate Your Products

Selecting a design and deciding on the basic construction materials of your permanent and temporary display fixtures are just the first step to creating an appealing environment from which to showcase and sell featured goods and services. The next step involves a bit of showmanship and imagination, since the presentation of products and the

props used to complement your merchandise display have a big impact on catching the shopper's attention and drawing the customer over for a closer look.

It should be obvious that just laying products flat on a table or piling them on shelves isn't the best way to display them.

Yet, many retailers do just that; then wonder why things aren't selling. One of the most important principles of good product presentation is elevation. Dimension and depth can be added to your display and products can be placed closer to eye level by elevating them in a variety of ways.

Any number of methods can be used to add height to your products and give your display area extra impact. An assortment of cardboard boxes, plastic containers, upside-down flower pots, crates, bricks, tiles or wooden boards can provide a variety of different levels on which to place your products.

Retailers with merchandise that has a rustic look, can use crates or bricks in their natural state to elevate and display their items and enhance the theme of their display. Fabric draped over boxes or brightly painted containers are effective props that elevate merchandise. Merchants selling portable phone systems or some other sophisticated merchandise, might use plexiglass risers or mirrored cubes to display their goods. Just use your imagination and plan out a display theme consistent with your merchandise and the expectations of your customer.

Use Props

Every retailer should go to the nearest regional shopping mall and spend an afternoon each month looking at the display windows and temporary exhibits and make notes on how props are used by window and store display designers. Props can create a theme, add impact, demonstrate usage, and provide functional assistance in presenting products to their best advantage. When props are used to help create a theme, they provide continuity and allow products to be displayed in a cohesive, well-blended manner.

For example, a retailer who sells hand-woven, wool sweaters and shawls might place an authentic weaver's loom in the middle of the sales area as the focal point. Sweaters can be displayed from the drawers of an antique pine dresser, on an antique dressmaker's dummy or stacked in an old, open trunk.

Likewise, a store selling dolls could use baby doll furniture as props. Displaying a doll in a rocking chair, high chair or cradle would add an appealing touch to the display and capture the shopper's interest. One independent bookseller put an antique, full-sized sleigh in the store as part of its

Christmas display to promote the purchase of books as the ideal holiday gift. Sales increased 15 percent over the same period the year prior.

Containers also make great props. They can be integrated throughout a display and filled with selected merchandise.

Baskets, barrels, crates, flower pots, fish bowls, mugs, trunks and brass pots are just a few containers that have been successfully incorporated into merchandise displays. Colorful tissue placed in containers also produces a dramatic effect.

For props to have impact, they must be creative, even outrageous! Retailers who sell jewelry or sunglasses, for example, might consider covering a display table with sand and beach towels and have items draped over interesting pieces of driftwood or coming out of beautiful sea shells.

A terrific display was developed by a woman who sells recharged laser printer cartridges at a considerable discount off the price of new ones. Because the product itself does not make an attractive or interesting display piece, the retailer had to think of some way to catch the attention of people passing by her store. Her window design was extremely creative, effective and low-cost. From a solid color backdrop, she fashioned a waterfall of oversized $100 bills cascading into a trash can. A sign read "WHY THROW YOUR MONEY AWAY?" Since her customers are business owners interested in cutting expenses, her window attracted immediate attention and provided an opening for her to explain how recharged cartridges could save money.

Demonstrations

Another way to gain attention is to display a product in use. Show customers what they can do with the product after they make the purchase. For example, create a breeze from a fan to demonstrate the sounds of wind chimes. Stained glass ornaments can be displayed by hanging them from a lighted Christmas tree, a window pane or a fireplace mantel. Hand-woven baskets can be filled with fruit, letters, condiments and bath products. A hand-blown vase can be filled with flowers, potpourri, or colored marbles. Painted silk scarfs can be tied around a hat or displayed as a belt.

Customer demonstrations on video tape for use with counter monitors are sometimes available from vendors. They can be very useful in capturing customer attention.

Showing the customer exactly how the product is used and how the shopper will benefit from its purchase can dramatically increase sales. One department store shows a video in the accessory department that demonstrated how to tie fashion scarves. Sales of silk scarves increased 50 percent when the video demonstration was running. Video presentations can be very helpful when demonstrating products that are too small, too large, too complicated, too time-consuming or too dangerous to demonstrate in the store by the sales staff.

Props that provide functional assistance can help facilitate the sale of products. Retailers who sell clothing should have a full-length mirror in the sales area, as well as in the dressing rooms. A hand-held mirror to view jewelry and earrings, a stool to sit on while trying on shoes, a tape player to hear seminar tapes, or tissues to wipe off makeup samples are examples of functional props necessary to provide assistance to the customer and help sell products. Some props are decorative and some are functional. Take time to consider which type would enhance the display of your merchandise and improve your selling opportunities.

Theme Merchandise And Holiday Packaging

Profits can be increased tremendously if vendors develop product lines that revolve around the themes of holidays and special events. Whenever possible, stock special items that will tie into a specific holiday season. If this is not possible, consider packaging what you offer in a creative way that reflects the holiday or decorating a display area in the holiday theme. For example, give a

carnation with each purchase on Valentine's Day and a chocolate rose on Mother's Day. Gift wrap your products in holiday papers. Add sparklers to the package for the Fourth of July or a green clover for St. Patrick's Day. Decorating themes for displays also can come from current events. Remember how effectively American flags and yellow ribbons were used to lure customers during the Persian Gulf War? Special items and theme packaging attract customers and encourage them to buy. Below is a list of some of the occasions and holiday themes to plan for as part of your merchandising effort.

Valentine's Day	St. Patrick's Day
Easter	Tax Season
Mother's Day	Father's Day
July Fourth	Back to School
Halloween	Thanksgiving
Hanukkah	Christmas
New Years	President's Day
Labor Day	New Baby
Marriages	Graduation
Communion	Birthdays
Anniversaries	Elections

Use Color Consistently

Businesses using specific colors and distinguishing logos to identify the company should use the same colors and logo in the design of their temporary displays, if appropriate. Consistent use of color is an effective way to gain name recognition and company identification, especially for companies who are in a very competitive category.

When choosing color to accent your temporary display and table coverings, pick colors that contrast with your products but do not clash with the overall store decor. Blue, black and red are good choices, but always select colors that will enhance the products. Avoid fabrics with busy patterns. Solid colors never detract from the product. Children's items are displayed best with pastels or bright primary colors. Jewelry and sculpture sell better when displayed against a black background. Black, navy and gray are colors that are more sophisticated and give a business-like impression.

Lighting

Most retailers believe that lighting affects sales; more light equals more sales. The question is, how many more sales will be produced for the cost of additional lighting? Determine if lighting is essential to your product presentation. Retailers selling fine art or intricate items with lots of detail, find they need spotlights to illuminate the work and help customers appreciate the quality of the craftsmanship or artistry.

Some stores with low general light, supplement the overhead lighting to increase the illumination of specific floor space. For spotlighting, the clip-on fixtures with concave, aluminum reflector shells work best. These can be clipped onto frames, shelves, tables or overhead piping. Carefully consider what lighting is important for your merchandising needs before you invest in any fixtures. If your electrical needs are extensive, you may wish to seek professional help in designing lighting for the store.

If lighting is essential, purchase the best quality fixtures you can afford. Durable, well-made equipment that can withstand time is a wise investment.

Keep It Neat And Clean

The importance of keeping the entire store clean and the merchandise displays neat and attractive cannot be over stated. Nothing turns off customers like a dirty, messy retail store. If you want customers to keep coming back and to enjoy their shopping experience, make sure every employee understands the need to pitch-in to keep the store looking its best.

Summary

For merchandise to stand out, it must be displayed to create impact. Impact is achieved by carefully planning the details of the store's merchandise display areas and incorporating the following:

* A theme to attract attention.

* Color identification for easy recognition.

* Methods to elevate your products.

* Props to enhance product presentation.

* Professional signs if needed.

* Adequate lighting to illuminate the merchandise.

* A neat and clean sales floor.

CHAPTER FIVE

Sharpen Your Sales Skills

Each time you open your doors, it costs time and money. Therefore, successful retail entrepreneurs must attempt to get the maximum return for their investment.

Set Goals For Sales

To help your business succeed, set concrete goals to accomplish every day. Goal setting directs your efforts and gives purpose to your actions. When store owners and sales staff have several goals to achieve, they have more chances to succeed. The primary reason for operating a store is to sell products and make money. Other worthwhile goals during a day's operation might include:

1. Building a mailing list of potential customers.

2. Introducing new products and assessing consumer reaction.

3. Gathering market information by talking to shoppers and identifying needs and wants.

4. Obtaining new sales leads.

5. Meeting suppliers, distributors, and other vendors that can help build the business.

6. Recruiting sales personnel.

7. Building public recognition for your store and its product lines.

8. Educating the buying public about your merchandise.

9. Gaining exposure for your business, while improving your sales skills.

Always make a list of goals to accomplish each week and share them with your staff. Next, take time for everyone to brush up on sales skills.

Whether the shop sells crafts or computers, developing an effective sales presentation is fundamental to the success of the store. Sales experts maintain that merchants must grab the attention of a shopper in 3.5 seconds. So, a well-conceived plan of attack is absolutely essential. Displays should be designed to attract shoppers. But even with exceptional displays, sales will not occur if the staff is unable to communicate product information that is informative, professional and persuasive, once the customer enters the store.

A retail business revolves around selling. Money is made only when something is sold. Therefore, owners and employees must become comfortable with the selling process in order to succeed. Unfortunately, many merchants love to surround themselves with products they enjoy, but hate to sell them. Much of the dislike for selling is derived from the notion that good salespeople must be aggressive and pushy.

With some preparation and practice, anyone can improve their selling skills and become comfortable making sales presentations without changing character or resorting to high-pressure selling tactics.

Project A Professional Image

Never underestimate the impact personality and appearance has on one's selling abilities and the store's profits. Getting one chance to make a first impression applies to every employee and owner. The overall image you and your staff project will determine whether a shopper will remain in your store or slip out the door. Selling yourself, by using methods that influence the customer's perception of you, can contribute to a shopper's willingness to buy.

Clothes That Make The Sale

The typical retailer thinks mostly of comfort when dressing for a day's work. This is often evidenced by the casual, and sometimes sloppy, appearance of their attire and grooming. A quick examination of the store personnel at a shopping center, for example, proves the point that some make a better impression than others. Those that project the most appealing image have dressed to complement their store image, dressed in the clothing they sell, or dressed in the style of the shopper's expectations.

A sales person who dresses to complement the store atmosphere, wears clothing that enhances the appeal of the merchandise or emphasizes the theme or image of the shop. For example, the female sales staff of a store selling country crafts could wear vintage style dresses or a country apron with the store's logo monogramed on the front. Someone selling medical or health supplies may choose to wear a lab coat. A sports equipment store may have all the floor staff wear matching sports wear. One well know athletic shoe store chain has the sales staff dress as referees in black and white stripped shirts and black pants. They even go so far as to have the staff wear a whistle around their necks.

Store owners that use imagination in selecting what the floor staff will wear can give their shop the extra impact that could provide a competitive edge. If it is possible to wear what you sell, by all means do it. Earrings, jewelry, clothing, shoes, belts, hats and scarves are just a few of the items owners and sales staff can model.

Your personnel should dress according to the image or theme of the store and the expectations of the customers. It can be conservative and businesslike, fashionable and sophisticated or casual and sporty. How employees dress for work can have an impact on how your store is perceived by the customers. So, matching work attire to the tastes of the customers could increase sales.

For example, a boutique offering fashionable, expensive clothing hopes to attract women shoppers who buy and wear expensive, fashionable clothing. The owner and sales staff will not inspire confidence in their fashion expertise if they are dressed in badly worn, shabby and outdated clothing.

Don't overlook the obvious. Pay careful attention to good hygiene and personal grooming, and no matter what style of dress your store selects, make sure everyone on the floor wears comfortable shoes.

A Professional Attitude

Successful sales people must convey a friendly and helpful attitude. To make money selling merchandise, the sales staff must enjoy dealing with people. Being pleasant to the customer is elementary, yet it is surprising how many people send out negative signals telegraphing their dislike for dealing with people.

To maintain a professional attitude, the staff also should be prepared to respond to unhappy customers occasionally. Decide in advance how you will handle returns or how you will deal with unpleasant and demanding customers. Although unpleasant incidents are rare, if anticipated and discussed, the staff will know what to do or say when they occur. Always be prepared to handle these situations calmly and diplomatically.

Happy customers can be the source of substantial referral business. So, give some thought to your return policy and how you will deal with an unsatisfied customer. Studies show that unhappy customers will tell twice as many friends negative things about a business as happy customers tell positive things. It's human nature for people to complain more than to compliment. Since complaints can kill sales quickly, plan your responses carefully.

Remember to be friendly, but not too aggressive; informative, but not pushy; enthusiastic, but not overbearing. Experience will help you and your staff find the best selling personality.

Using Body Language To Your Advantage

Studies show that men and women send out certain strong messages just by the way they sit, stand or posture themselves.

Standing with your arms crossed, for example, sends out a message to "keep your distance, don't come too close." Sale people can appear more approachable by keeping their arms at their sides or behind their back.

Making eye contact with potential customers projects warmth and friendliness. Try to catch the eye of all potential customers that come in the store to look at merchandise. Then, greet them with a smile and a simple, "Hello" or "How are you doing today?" One study showed that by simply changing the greeting from "may I help you?" to "have you been in our store before?" can increase sales 17 percent. Why? Because everyone says, "May I help you?" and most without an ounce of sincerity.

Avoid reading or occupying yourself with anything that does not pertain directly to merchandising. If you look too busy and don't acknowledge the customer's presence immediately, it is unlikely shoppers will approach you with questions. You will lose a chance to engage the prospect in conversation and qualify the person as a potential buyer.

On the other hand, do not look too idle, either. Busy yourself by straightening the stock or adding up receipts. Don't stand by the door looking as if you are ready to pounce on the first person that shows the slightest interest.

Today's buyers are on guard, and most resent the overly aggressive salesperson. Successful selling begins when the salesperson is able to tell the response and comfort level of the prospect by observing the shopper's body language.

Here is a simple technique you can use when the customer becomes uncomfortable as you approach the close of a sale. Take several steps backward or move away from the customer and busy yourself with something for a moment. Straighten a display or put something into the waste basket. Watch the reactions of the customer and listen to the tone of voice. You will be amazed at how effective this gesture is for putting customers at ease and for letting them feel they are in control of the purchasing decision.

The study of body language has been the subject of many books and articles. Make some observations, read about the subject and incorporate what you learn in your selling methods. You will find applying this knowledge can make a difference in your sales effectiveness.

Your Sales Presentation

Think of selling as the art of persuasive conversation. Learning what to say, as well as how and when to say it, is the key to increasing your sales and profits. Effective selling is really very simple. Just remember the three E's of successful selling: ENGAGE, EXCITE, ENCOURAGE. You're probably thinking, "Sure, that sounds easy, but what exactly do I say?"

To start with, you cannot sit behind your counter patiently waiting for customers to come over and ask you to ring up the sale. Some people actually believe their merchandise will sell itself. That's occasionally true, but research shows that initiating and following through with the proper selling process will generate many more sales.

Preparation is essential. To be comfortable with and capable at selling, you must be prepared. A sales presentation given by an accomplished salesperson generally follows a pattern. First, the salesperson approaches the prospect casually and starts a conversation with small talk. Then, the salesperson proceeds to gain the potential customer's confidence while informing them of the product's assets in an unassuming manner. Through a series of questions and answers, the salesperson qualifies the prospect. Finally, the salesperson directs the customer to buy.

The sales presentation can be memorized and should vary from prospect to prospect only slightly. The best selling presentations are those that influence customers to buy, yet leave them pleased and satisfied that the decision to buy was their own.

Develop an effective presentation by writing down what you wish to say to each potential customer. Next, memorize the presentation word for word. Practice with your family and friends until you feel confident and comfortable with what you are saying. Lack of attention to the basics often is the reason many fail to succeed in sales. Stick to the presentation and use it consistently with all prospects.

A good salesperson must be attentive to the customer. This doesn't mean pouncing on everyone that comes within two feet of the merchandise. It means keeping your eyes on their eyes. You are looking for the person who hesitates in front of a display, stares at a product from across the aisle, approaches with curiosity or stops to pick up an item. These cues indicate the customer wants to know more about the products.

When you notice these behaviors, it's time to make the critical first move to ENGAGE the prospect in a conversation and qualify the person as a potential buyer. Never start the conversation by saying, "May I help you?" The automatic response usually is, "No thanks, just looking."

Instead, use what I call "SHOPPER STOPPERS." Shopper stoppers are special questions or statements that compel the customer to stay and talk with you. First, make eye contact, then say something like, "Hi, have you been in our store before?"

When politely responded to, you might say, "These T-shirts are 100 percent cotton and preshrunk."

Or, "These handbags were hand tooled in Italy. I selected them on my buying trip there last month. They are so unusual. What color are you looking for?"

Or, "How old is the child you have in mind for this toy? We carry toys suitable for children one through four in this section."

Or, "These are machine washable; do you like the plain or flowered ones?"

Staffers selling handmade jewelry or custom-designed earrings might say, "I'll bet you've never seen anything like these new mother of pearl earrings before. Do you wear the pierced or the clip-on type?"

Or, "All our jewelry is handmade by Native Americans. This piece is from the Zuni tribe."

Or, "I carry both pierced and clip-on earrings. What shape are you looking for?"

Or, "This new computer model features a backlit screen and a modem; let me show you how great this works."

These are just a few examples of opening lines that attempt to ENGAGE customers and either make them stop and talk more, which indicates that a sale is possible, or force them to quickly answer and move on, which means they weren't interested and you saved yourself a lot of time.

Always remember merchandising is done for the purpose of making sales. Be sure you have interested, qualified customers before you take up your time and their time giving a sales presentation. Many people will be just browsing. If you spend time repeating the presentation to everyone, without thought to the prospect's financial ability to buy, timing, authority to purchase or desire for the products, you will wear yourself out and generate very few sales. Every person pursued should be a qualified buyer. With a little experience, potential customers can be spotted easily.

After the prospect has been qualified and shows continued interest, a successful salesperson moves on to step two, EXCITE! When appropriate, put the product in the customer's hands. Let them feel it, try it on or see how it works. Confirm that you have the right size, the right color and you can ship anywhere, if that's what it takes to make the sale. Offer information of interest that will create desire for your product. If you are selling something made by hand, tell the prospect how difficult it is to make, discuss the rarity of the materials used or the uniqueness of the design. If a vendor is a local artist, designer, inventor or crafter who made the item, the sales staff should mention this to the prospect.

Product Knowledge Is Essential

If you are an exclusive retailer of a product line or the buyer who travels to Hong Kong and personally selects each item, be sure to inform the shopper. Enthusiasm sells, but product knowledge sells more. So, take pride in your work and learn as much as possible about the products you are merchandising in the store.

If your store sells a business product or personal service, you should demonstrate the benefits of the offerings. Show prospects what the service will do for them. Explain the extent of the warranty and tell why the product is better than others on the market. Indicate when delivery is possible; talk about quality and demonstrate performance.

When you feel prospects are convinced of what they need and want and what you offer, proceed to step three. ENCOURAGE them to buy it, now. A simple, closing statement like, "May I wrap that up for you?" or "Let me show you our best payment schedule," will either result in the sale or bring up an objection. When potential customers present objections, they are saying "sell me more!"

The entire persuasive conversation or sales presentation takes only a matter of minutes. Here is an example of a sales presentation for personalized children's books.

A woman glances toward a display of books. The salesperson attempts to ENGAGE her with a SHOPPER STOPPER.

"Do you have a special little one to buy for?" The prospect nods yes and stops to get a closer look.

The salesperson opens the book and hands it to her explaining, "Your favorite child is the star of the story. We customize each book right here in just four minutes."

The customer looks intrigued and asks, "What age group are these appropriate for?"

This is the time to EXCITE the prospect and continue to build interest. The salesperson explains, "They are perfect for children 12 years of age and under. Each book includes the child's name, age, city, family, and friends in the story. How old is the child you have in mind?"

She replies, "My grandson is turning seven."

The customer is excited and qualified, so an attempt is made to ENCOURAGE her to buy now. "I recommend *The Lost Dinosaur*; little boys just love the story."

The sales person hands her the selection and says, "All you need to do is fill out this form and I can make the book for you in four minutes."

The skilled salesperson always assumes the customer will buy, and behaves as if it's only a matter of time until the transaction takes place.

Why People Buy

There are two reasons why shoppers make purchases. First, because they are attracted to the product or service. The second reason, and many times the real reason the sale is made, is because the customer likes the salesperson. Salespeople who are always friendly, helpful and informative can influence how customers feel about their products. People enjoy buying from salespeople who are excited about what they sell and who enjoy their work. Enthusiasm often can compensate for a lack of sales expertise.

In addition, shoppers often will buy a product simply because they discovered something in common with the salesperson. To increase sales, always try to find a common bond with prospects. During a sales presentation you may discover you're both from the same hometown, your kids go to the same school, or you both have a Labrador Retriever.

Believe it or not, these personal links often can be the reason a customer will buy from you and not from your competitor. While trying to establish a link, never be too pushy or too talkative, and never get upset if you don't make the sale.

Overcoming Objections

Even if you are friendly and informative and able to give a great sales pitch, not every potential customer will be an easy sell. A person may hesitate to buy because an item is too expensive, too small, too large, not the right color, or a myriad of other reasons. These objections usually don't surface directly. Probe for objections throughout your conversation and listen for clues that will uncover the reasons shoppers are hesitating. When someone gives you an objection, remember they really are telling you "sell me more."

When you think you know what is preventing the prospect from making the purchase, confront him with it. If you think the problem is price, you might say, "I have several payment schedules available with no interest for six months. Which of these plans sound good to you?" The customer, at this point, might reveal the true problem. "I have to consult my partners first before I make this purchase." If you think the problem is color or size and you can provide other choices not displayed, you might say, "I can get these dresses in blue or yellow, too. Were you looking for a different color?" The customer, at this point, might reveal the true problem, like "My daughter has so many dresses, she really needs pants."

Learning to overcome objections is a very important part of your sales presentation. After developing your sales pitch, make a list of every excuse a customer might use for not purchasing your merchandise. Next, write down what you will say as a rebuttal to each objection. Memorize your rebuttals and be prepared to use them when the customer presents an objection.

Sales professionals claim it takes six attempts to close a sale before the sale is made. The reason many people fail at sales is not because they can't sell, it's because they quit too soon. Wait until the customer gives says "no" five times. More than likely, your sixth try will close the sale.

Selling is an art. The more you and your sales staff learn about selling, the more you can earn for your business. Don't underestimate the need to acquire knowledge and expertise in selling. Read as many books on the subject as you can. Attend workshops and seminars to improve selling skills. Observe and imitate other merchants who have excellent sales skills. The extra effort will pay off and help your business grow and prosper.

Add-On Selling

The next time you eat at a fast food restaurant listen carefully to what the cashier says after you place an order. You probably will be asked if you would like an order of fries or a soft drink to go with your meal. This seemingly simple gesture is a calculated sales technique. It's one of the reasons why McDonald's is the leader in the fast food trade. All competitors now follow suit, but McDonald's pioneered the technique of the add-on sale. The goal of add-on selling is to get every customer to buy more than they originally intended.

By simply suggesting the customer might like a pair of colored laces to go with the new, hand-painted shoes or a computer dust jacket for the new laptop computer, a merchant may be able to increase the dollar amount of the sale substantially. Another way to encourage additional purchases is to offer a second item at a discount. When you are adding up the purchases at the register or writing out the sales receipt, mention a second item can be purchased at a discount off the regular price. Train yourself to always think in terms of add-on sales. Combine, match, pair or accessorize as many products as you can. You will be surprised how this will increase the dollar amount of each sale. Since you already have an interested customer, who is ready to make one purchase, it is easier to sell more to that customer than to start over with another one.

CHAPTER SIX

Ideas For Making More Money

Some retailers have found they can make additional money by reaching out to customers who cannot or will not come to the store to shop. To do this successfully, however, requires careful planning, preparation and execution.

Simply put, the idea is to find ways to attract and serve customers who will never step through the doors of your store, or to continue to sell to past customers who no longer find it convenient to shop at your establishment.

Before you decide to implement any outreach sales and merchandising program, be sure to carefully study your customer. Develop a typical, preferred customer profile. Determine the age, sex, education, income level, residential location and buying habits of the type of customer that purchases your merchandise. Then, find out in advance if your type of customer is likely to come in contact with your merchandise through the type of outreach methods you are considering. Some typical outreach methods are described in this chapter. Determine if any would work for your retail business.

Exhibit Marketing At Weekend Events

Many retailers have found they can make extra money from their retail business by exhibit marketing at weekend events. Thousands of craft fairs, trade shows, farmers' markets and civic and community events take place every weekend. In addition, there are hundreds of other events and locations where enterprising retailers can exhibit and sell merchandise.

Exhibit marketing started hundreds of years ago at bazaars and open markets where people gathered to buy and sell food and merchandise. Today, these temporary selling venues constitute one of the fastest growing segments of the retail industry, attracting millions of shoppers who spend billions of dollars. Most of these venues have a festival atmosphere and are viewed as a social or entertainment excursion, as well as a shopping experience.

These events can provide excellent selling opportunities for the retailer willing to take merchandise out of the store to reach more customers. Retailers must match their products with the purposes and theme of the events and the audiences they are likely to reach. A sample list of locations and events that have money making potential follows:

Antique Shows	Grand Openings
Balloon Festivals	Conventions
Rodeos	Baby Fairs
Carnivals	Parenting Groups
Auctions	Gift Shows
Block Parties/Festivals	Flea Markets
Swap Meets	Sporting Events
Community Celebrations	Car Shows
Wine Tastings	State and County Fairs
Church Events	Charity Events
Air Shows	School Functions

Opportunities to show and sell merchandise are everywhere. Resourceful retailers always will be looking for places to apply exhibit marketing skills.

Select shows and fairs that you believe can generate substantial profit from the sale of your particular merchandise. Then, understand the elements that must be present to minimize risk and maximize profits. When you identify the elements of a successful weekend retailing opportunity, you will feel more comfortable picking those that will be most profitable.

Typically, the elements to consider are as follows:

Customer Traffic - Will the event generate sufficient traffic to make the effort worthwhile?

Audience - Will the vast majority of those attending the event be your type of customer?

Location - Is the location convenient to your customer base?

Operating Hours - Will the event take place during times when it is convenient for your type of customer to attend?

Show Promoter - Who is producing and promoting the event and what is the company's track record for success?

Competing Events - Are other events competing at the same time for the same audience?

Entry Fees - Are the entry fees attractive enough to make participation viable?

Publicity - How are the show promoters planning to publicize the event and attract your type of customer?

The main purpose of participating in these events is to sell your merchandise on the spot. Another reason for considering this approach, however, is to use the event as a vehicle to advertise your permanent retail store to new, potential customers who see and like what you offer. If you want to try exhibit marketing at a location outside your store, there are a number of things to keep in mind.

Your Exhibit Space

The amount of display space assigned to an exhibitor and its location at the event site will vary greatly from show to show. Promoters of large events usually provide a map showing numbered booth spaces from which exhibitors choose an exact location. Space is sold on a first come, first serve basis. Typically, each space measures approximately 10-feet by 10-feet. If necessary, exhibitors can buy an adjacent booth space, remove the center divider, and have a 10-foot by 20-foot selling area. Sometimes show promoters offer a discount on the purchase of more than one space.

Corner spaces are desirable because they provide exposure to customers from two sides. Promoters charge a premium for corner spots, because the additional exposure usually means additional sales. Corner booths can be worth the extra expense, especially if you have popular items to sell.

Exhibitors often disagree about the best booth locations at a show site. Some exhibitors like being near the entrance. Others prefer the areas near the food and entertainment, places where crowds gather. Personally, it's best to avoid booths near the entrance, because many buyers are reluctant to purchase the first things they see. Shoppers usually prefer to view most of the offerings first, before making their purchases. Spots near food or entertainment concessions have drawbacks, too. People gathering there are occupied with eating or watching the entertainment. In addition, the noise level near these areas often is too loud to give a sales presentation properly. It's safest to choose a booth located in the middle of the exhibit arena, whenever possible.

The large craft fairs and trade shows offer booth spaces that come with an 8-foot back drape and 3-foot side drapes to separate each exhibitor. Usually a 6-foot or 8-foot display table, chair and waste basket are provided as part of the exhibiting package and included as part of the entry fee.

A convention service, contracted by the show promoter, provides the draped booths. A variety of additional display items such as racks, shelves, easels and pegboards can be rented through the convention service. Plants, flowers, carpeting, table covers and other decorator items also are available for rent. Cleaning services and electrical outlets can be obtained for an additional fee.

At small shows and local craft fairs, booth set up is unpredictable. Where a display is placed depends on how early the exhibitor arrives to set up and how much space the display requires. This casual approach to space planning can be advantageous to the clever weekend retailer. Since boundaries of each exhibit are not very distinct, exhibitors often can spread their products throughout the show. If permitted by the promoter, integrating merchandise into the exhibits of other vendors can be a successful display technique that makes everything look attractive to the shoppers. Regardless of where exhibitors wish to place their displays, the promoter always has the final say about location assignments and displaying of merchandise.

The Show Schedule

Typically, craft fairs and trade shows open at 9 a.m. and close at 5 p.m. Some shows and meets operate during the evening. Most shows are one to four days in length. Thursdays through Sundays are the most popular days of the week for shows. Exhibitors often are required to set up all equipment and displays the day before the show opens. Always arrive early on opening day. Your exhibit should be in place and you should be ready for business at least one hour before the show officially opens. Use this time to look over other exhibits and survey the competition.

Don't underestimate the importance of setting up your display early. Successful exhibitors need time to relax and get into a positive frame of mind before shoppers arrive. Nothing is more frustrating than arriving late and rushing to set up the display, while hundreds of potential buyers pass by your booth.

Exhibitors are not permitted to break down their exhibits until the show officially closes. Sometimes an exhibitor's contract requires that vendors wait until all customers have left the selling area before dismantling displays. Fines have been levied against exhibitors who disregarded this rule. Follow this simple request if you want to maintain a good business relationship with the promoters.

Fire Regulations

Most shows require exhibitors to comply with strict fire safety rules and regulations established by local authorities. Be safe and make sure all display materials are fire retardant. The district Fire Marshal often does on-site, random flame tests at most shows. This means the Marshal may come to your booth and place a lighted match to the bottom of your table covering to see if it will burn.

If you employ a professional design company to make your table covering, ask the designer to use flame retardant materials. You also can apply a variety of spray-on or wash-in, flame retardant products to your exhibit materials or hire a company to do it for you. Look in the Yellow Pages under "flameproofing" for companies specializing in this service and at the hardware stores for the self-application products. Consult the Fire Marshal in your area for complete information regarding fire safety rules and regulations.

Lighting

Most retailers believe that lighting affects sales; more light equals more sales. The question is, how many more sales will be produced for the cost of additional lighting? At most shows, electrical connections available at the booth space will cost an additional $35 to $50, and lighting fixtures can cost several hundred dollars.

Determine if lighting is essential to your product presentation. Vendors selling fine art or intricate items with lots of detail, find they need spotlights to illuminate the work and help customers appreciate the quality of the craftsmanship.

Some vendors exhibiting indoors with low light, supplement the overhead lighting to increase the illumination of the entire booth space. Most indoor shows, however, are held in large exhibit halls with excellent lighting. In addition, shows held outdoors during the day usually require no additional lighting.

Most promoters limit a vendor's power allotment to 500 watts. Eight, 60-watt bulbs will provide adequate lighting for a 10-foot by 10-foot booth. For spotlighting, the clip-on fixtures with concave, aluminum reflector shells work best.

These can be clipped onto frames, shelves, tables or overhead piping. Carefully consider what lighting is important for your display needs before you invest in any fixtures.

Getting Organized

The smart weekend retailer knows the advantages of preparing for each exhibiting event several days in advance. Careful attention to details prevents costly mistakes, like forgetting the cash box, neglecting to pack advertising literature or leaving behind the tools necessary to erect your display. Checklists of your inventory and supplies will ensure against such disasters.

Start by making a complete list of all the products you will sell at each exhibiting event. Create a list that categorizes each item by color, size, style or other descriptive characteristics that can help you track inventory after each show. Use this list as a sales record. Not only will it help you with restocking and reordering merchandise, it will make it easy to evaluate which items did or did not sell at each event.

Separate all the items you will bring to each event into categories such as display materials, sales literature, cashiering supplies, tools, personal necessities and product inventory. Make a checklist of every item in each category down to the last paper clip, then make copies of each. Plastic tubs and heavy cardboard boxes are excellent containers for storing and transporting your merchandise and supplies. Place the list of contents on the outside of each container. Check off items as you fill each container with one category of supplies.

Purchase a heavy-duty hand truck or cart for transporting your display and supplies from your vehicle to the show site. Sometimes the walk is quite long, so the fewer trips the better.

Include several large sheets of heavy, clear plastic in your supplies. The type of plastic sheets found at paint and hardware stores, commonly used as painter's drop cloths, work well. If it rains while you are working an outdoor show, the clear plastic sheets will protect the merchandise from getting wet and still allow customers to see what is offered.

Bring your own food. The food sold at most weekend events is usually overpriced and unhealthy. Since most exhibitors work at least eight hours, pack some healthy meals and plenty of fruit and snacks to sustain your energy.

Load your vehicle the evening before the show to eliminate the possibility of forgetting something in the morning rush to get on the road. Plan enough time to have coffee or to eat breakfast before you leave the house, so you can relax and get into a positive frame of mind on your way to the event.

Be A Prepared Exhibitor

Inventory your supplies and mark off each item on the checklist attached to each supply container to guard against forgetting essentials. Then, pack your merchandise and supplies in the easy-to-carry containers and load your vehicle the evening before the event.

For a display to be practical for exhibit marketing, it also must be:

* Able to fit into your vehicle.
* Easy to transport from your vehicle to your display area.
* Lightweight.
* Simple to assemble.
* Quick to break down.
* Durable to withstand repeat use.

You may find only one or two such events in your community worth the time and effort required to bring a temporary display and merchandise out of the store and into the path of potential new customers. Nevertheless, if carefully selected, these opportunities can add significant revenue to your business by allowing you to sell lots of merchandise to eager shoppers and by making more customers aware of your permanent location.

Carts And Kiosks

If you want to reach customers at another location but are not ready to open another store, try selling your merchandise from a specialty vendor cart or a kiosk. These mini-stores can be located in large regional shopping malls, airport terminals, sports arenas, street corners and other semi-permanent locations.

You can build and own your mini-store or, in some cases, rent the carts and kiosks from mall managers. Short-term rentals allow you to try a new location without major risk.

Determine if your merchandise can be properly displayed and sold from carts or kiosks. Then, determine what locations may be suitable for expanding your merchandising effort beyond your store.

Mail Order

A customer list is the most valuable marketing tool you can have. Inexpensive personal computers make it almost effortless to develop and maintain a customer list that can help you generate more sales from your retail store.

Always make sure you get the name and mailing address of every customer that makes a purchase. One way to gather this information is from customer checks. In addition, code your data base to identify the types of products each customer buys from your store. Armed with this information, you can generate additional sales by sending out product lists and mini-catalogs to your customer base. Offer a mail order service for those unwilling to stop by the store.

Personal Shopper

Your customer data base can help you provide extraordinary customer service by adding the personal touch to the shopping experience. For example, always ask each shopper what they are looking for. If it is not available, offer to contact them when the merchandise they may be interested in arrives at your store.

In addition, your best customers will develop shopping patterns. Make sure you record purchases in your data base so you can alert customers about merchandise they may wish to purchase. Offer to seek out special merchandise for your best customers. Keep the information updated in your data bank.

A personalized shopping experience cannot be found in large department stores and discount outlets. Customers who feel the merchant is working on behalf of satisfying their needs will keep coming back for more.

Telephone Sales

Again, because a personal computer can track customers and their purchasing habits, you can use your customer list to stimulate sales by telephone. When things are slow on the floor, the sales staff should be on the telephone talking to customers. Armed with information about past purchases, the sales staff can let customers know that similar or complimentary merchandise is available. Or, that a preferred customer sale will be held the night before a sale opens to the public.

The telephone can be used to build a relationship with the customer, if it is done in a way that makes the customer feel the call is to provide a service and not just to sell something.

Retail merchants must look for ways to expand their business to take fuller advantage of the marketplace. Sitting in the store and waiting for customers to come in may not be enough for the store to survive.

CHAPTER SEVEN

Low-cost Promotion For Your Retail Store

If you are like most small business owners, you probably are very uncomfortable with the whole idea of promoting your business. Don't worry, you are not alone. Frankly, most business owners feel much better about their ability to select merchandise, manage the employees, watch the cash flow and deliver the customer service, than they do about their ability to reach and motivate new customers through promotional activities.

Small business owners, and especially small retailers, often feel at a loss when it comes to business promotion. They realize that great sums of money can be wasted on efforts that produce little or no results. They seldom feel confident about selecting the right activities for their business. Some are so paralyzed by the fear they may lose money on promotional activities that they do little or nothing at all to promote their business. Others think only very creative people have the talent to be good at business promotion, or that it takes lots of money to have an effective program. Some think promotion can only be done right by marketing professionals, whose fees are beyond their reach.

This chapter should help to dispel many of these notions, as well as stress the importance of business promotion to the success of any company. Promotional activities play a key role in a company's marketing strategy. If you have carefully selected your target market, identified its needs, found merchandise to meet the needs, found ways to make it easy for your potential customers to get what you have to offer and priced your offerings so your prospects can afford them, you are ready for business success.

WHAT'S MISSING FROM THE ABOVE MENTIONED RECIPE? A key ingredient, promotion. If you don't let potential customers know about your store and its merchandise, you will never make as many sales as may be possible from your store.

In addition, how a company goes about promoting itself will have a tremendous impact on the identity and image the business has in the marketplace. So, careful attention must be placed on what methods and messages you select to attract potential customers.

Use Multiple Methods And Be Consistent

Seasoned business owners know that no single method of promotion will be enough to reach and motivate the vast majority of potential customers in their market territories. Therefore, the smart business owner will select 10-12 promotional activities to use on a consistent basis. The key to successful promotion on a small budget is consistency over a long period of time. A business must be consistent in the methods it uses to promote the business and the messages it sends to attract customers. That means successful business promotion requires a strong commitment to a realistic plan that invests adequate resources of time and money.

Promotional activities generally fall into one of five major categories:

Advertising

Packaging

Personal Sales

Public Relations/Publicity

Sales Incentives

In this chapter, each category is briefly explained and different promotional methods suitable for retailers are described. To help you develop a plan for promoting your business, follow these simple steps:

First, read through each of the various promotional methods and put a check mark next to those methods you think might work for your business.

Next, give more thought to each activity you checked and determine what your budget can afford and if your preferred customers will be reached and motivated by the methods you are considering.

Finally, select the best 10-12 methods and complete the chart at the end of the chapter. The chart will help you organize your promotional strategy over a one-year period.

Promoting your business can be both creative and fun, especially when ingenuity and resourcefulness are employed. The ideas in this chapter are tried and true methods used by thousands of successful small business owners. Many of the ideas should work for your business, too.

Advertising

What is advertising? Advertising is the PAID placement of a message or messages to promote the goods and services of a business. The company placing the advertising has complete control over the message used and the delivery system. The control is possible because the company is paying for the activity. Anytime you pay to deliver a message to your customers or potential customers, you are advertising.

Unfortunately, many small business owners waste their limited resources by not being careful about where, when or how they advertise. Since it is unlikely that small retailers will have the means to purchase large quantities of radio and TV air time and print advertising space and billboards, they may need to select more personal and direct methods to advertise their stores. Here are some simple tips to help you get the most out of your advertising efforts and your advertising dollars.

First, control your destiny. Don't become the prey of every advertising salesperson that comes along. With a simple and solid marketing strategy and promotion plan you won't become a victim of haphazard advertising. Haphazard advertising usually occurs when sales are slow and the business owner starts to panic. Suddenly, in walks an advertising salesperson with a "special" that can't be refused. The depressed retailer falls for the sales pitch, without really considering whether or not the advertising vehicle is right for the business. Moreover, the sales representative usually "helps" the shop owner create an ad right on the spot. Little planning or thought goes into the development of the ad. With this approach to advertising, the commissioned advertising salesperson is in control, not the business owner. As a result, the advertising usually produces few, if any, sales and the retailer complains that he/she tried advertising once and it just didn't work.

To avoid these occurrences, take charge of your advertising and promotion plan. If you plan your advertising and promotional activities, selecting those that are likely to reach and motivate your potential customers, you can let advertising sales representatives know that their offer just doesn't fit in with your marketing strategy. Most importantly, you will avoid spending your cash on advertising that doesn't work.

Second, choose your approach. Decide what you will emphasize in your advertising. Your approach should be one that you believe in and with which you are comfortable. If you don't believe in what you are presenting to the public, nobody else will.

To select your approach, remember the needs and wants of your preferred customer. Do they seek your merchandise because your store is convenient, your merchandise unique, your personal service extraordinary? Do they associate status or belonging, health or well-being, approval or self-esteem with your offerings? Do they come to your business because the service is friendly?

Examine your entire business, including the environment, service capability, facilities, dress of employees, and attitude toward the customer. Determine what you think makes your store different from your competition. Decide what you think is your biggest plus and see if your current customers agree. If so, that characteristic should be the thrust of your advertising approach. See if you can create an advertising slogan by describing your greatest business asset in ten words or less. Use your slogan, even if it is in small print, on all your advertising.

Third, select the media. To be effective, you must select more than one method to advertise your business. No single vehicle will reach and motivate all your prospects and customers. While all advertising will have the same approach, choosing the right media will be important. Select several methods to promote your business. You can select the right methods for your business from the various activities that are described later in this chapter. Repeat your advertising in the selected media as often as you can afford to do so.

Fourth, develop an advertising and promotion budget. There are several ways to determine an appropriate budget. Some of the more common ways are to determine a percentage of the operating budget, or a percentage of gross receipts to apply to advertising and promotion. Remember it is important to set aside some money, time and resources for marketing and advertising if you want your store to survive.

In the beginning, expect to spend about fifteen to twenty percent or more of gross receipts on marketing and advertising. Depending on the type of business you operate, that figure should drop to about five to ten percent once the customer base is firmly established.

Fifth, give your advertising and promotion plan time to work. A business owner should develop a plan that covers at least a full year. A simple way to organize a yearly plan is described at the end of this chapter. The owner must be willing to stick to the plan, making adjustments after six to eight months. With a small budget, it takes time for an advertising and promotion plan to show results. Be patient, there are no instant results. Think of your advertising and promotional activities as a snowball rolling down a hill, gaining size and momentum with each turn. You must give your plan time to work if you want to gain the benefits of consistent advertising and promotion.

Finally, be consistent. It is important that all advertising be consistent in message, methods and image. Make a commitment to one particular advertising approach and stick to it. Choose appropriate advertising and promotion vehicles, add your slogan, implement your advertising and promotion activities on a regular basis and follow your plan.

Here are several advertising ideas you can consider:

Co-op Advertising

Co-op advertising is advertising that shares its cost among several parties - usually the retailer, distributor and manufacturer. If you put the name of a product you sell in your ads, you may be able to negotiate with the manufacturer or supplier and get them to agree to share the cost of advertising with you. Sometimes, the supplier will be willing to split the cost 50/50 with the retailer. Ask for advertising support from the companies whose products and services you carry. Some newspapers even have a cooperative advertising department that assists a company in seeking ad money from suppliers. Cooperative advertising arrangements can go a long way to help the retailer get at least part of the advertising paid for by the supplier or manufacturer. For example, a specialty food store may get most of its advertising paid for by the suppliers of products it features in weekly ads. Every year millions of co-op dollars go unused. Retailers should find out if they qualify for co-op advertising dollars and use them to lower their advertising expense.

Magazine Advertising

Magazine ads tend to instill consumer confidence in the company or the product being advertised. Local magazines or regional editions of national magazines offer lower advertising rates. Also, you can run an ad once in a prestigious publication, have the ad reprinted, and use the reprint for several years as a flier. Because there are hundreds of specialty, local and trade magazines, magazine ads can be targeted directly to your audience sending your message to the most likely prospects. Magazines have a longer shelf life, so your ad may be viewed several times by the same reader. Also, because of the quality of the paper used in magazines, they are a better medium if you want to advertise in color.

Here's a way to save money with your magazine ads. Have a magazine size ad ready to go at all times. Tell the advertising representatives of the magazines you wish to use that you are a small business on a very tight budget and are interested in buying only last-minute, unsold space at greatly reduced rates. You may need to wait several editions, but you will save enormous amounts of money. If you use a prestigious local or national magazine to advertise your products, mention this in your other advertising vehicles, "As seen in....magazine."

Newspaper Ads

Always have your newspaper and print ads initially designed and produced by a capable graphic artist. No matter what the ad salesperson says, most newspaper ad departments are not able to produce effective display ads. Pay for the general design of a basic ad, with a window of space to insert information about your offers. Then, have it reproduced in several sizes or use it as a model for later ads produced by the paper. Also, good copy writing is essential to make your ad appealing and to make it stand out from the other ads. Be sure to run your ads on the right day and test the effectiveness of the various local newspapers you have selected by doing a coupon advertisement or special offer.

After you have given the newspapers a few months to test, drop the ones that do not draw. A good ad can be run over and over again; only you will become bored with it. On a small budget, it is unlikely you can run it often enough or large enough for complete saturation to occur. A good ad can last 2-3 years, especially if it is designed with a window to insert special offerings. Excellent ads also can be re-printed and used as statement stuffers, fliers, handouts, mailers or even enlarged and used as a poster.

Newspaper Inserts

Newspaper inserts often work better than display ads. You can produce your own sales sheets, fliers or mini-catalogs and have them inserted and delivered with a local newspaper. Usually, the advertiser must deliver the pre-printed materials to the newspaper at least one week in advance of distribution. Also, contact in advance the local advertising representative of the newspaper for any special requirements. Most often, the publisher will charge a few pennies per insert to deliver it with the newspaper. Inserts are especially effective when delivered with smaller, community newspapers that don't regularly carry large quantities of inserts.

An insert can really catch attention when it literally falls in the reader's lap. In addition, the interested reader can easily put the insert aside for future reference without having to cut up the newspaper. To test the effectiveness of this method, include a coupon, limited-time offer, or ask the customer to bring the insert to your place of business to register for a prize or receive a free gift or discount. Make sure the insert is eye catching and projects the appropriate image for your store.

Yellow Pages

Before signing a contract with a commissioned Yellow Pages sales representative, determine if your business will generate sales by placing an ad in the Yellow Pages larger than the standard courtesy line. Ask the question, do most people looking for merchandise such as yours consult the Yellow Pages to find it? Then call businesses similar to yours which are running display ads and ask the question, "I found you in the Yellow Pages; do most of your customers find you that way?" If the answer is "yes" and the Yellow Pages look promising, you can increase your response rate by carefully writing the ad copy and sizing your ad as large as your competitors. Since convenience is most important to consumers, set your telephone number and address in large type. Experts suggest you give as much information about your store as you can, without overcrowding the ad.

Ads are billed monthly to your phone bill and begin only after the Yellow Pages are published and delivered. There are many variations to the Yellow Pages. Use caution before placing an ad in competing directories. Most are not very effective and all are expensive. The Yellow Pages are popular because they have a reputation for being an effective advertising medium. That reputation has been reinforced by the advertising the company does to promote its directory. Moreover, everyone has heard of the Yellow Pages.

Some advertisers will get more results from each advertising dollar in the Yellow Pages than from any other advertising method. Even so, most business owners are dissatisfied with the results they get from the Yellow Pages. That's because Yellow Pages advertising does not create a desire on the part of the potential customer to buy. The Yellow Pages simply direct the customer, who is ready to buy, to the seller. While Yellow Pages advertising can generate new customers and clients, increase sales and add to the bottom line, too often dollars spent with the Yellow Pages are not used wisely.

To get the most from your Yellow Pages advertising dollar, don't depend on the Yellow Pages alone. You need to develop a cost-effective, total advertising and promotion plan to direct customers to your store. Then, when they are ready to buy, customers can easily find you in the Yellow Pages. However, never ask customers in your other advertising to look for you in the Yellow Pages. To do so simply courts disaster. When the prospect goes to the Yellow Pages to find you specifically, he will be confronted with all your competitors. He may decide to call or visit a competitor that is closer or to get price comparisons on the phone.

Radio

Radio advertising gives the business owner a chance to reach customers or clients with a spoken or musical message. Unlike print advertising that requires the prospect to read the message, radio advertising takes no effort on the part of the listener. Another advantage of radio is its ability to reach a more selected target market than newspapers, because different stations in large markets appeal to different audiences. To determine if radio will work for you, ask your current customers if they listen to the radio. If they answer yes, then ask them what stations they listen to and when. Before exploring radio further, it's a good idea to establish a profile of your preferred customer. Identify the demographic characteristics of your customer base and match it to the demographics of a station's listeners. Insist that the radio advertising sales representative provide you with accurate information about the station's audience and size. The station ad representative can send you the information.

Some stations will trade "air time" for products and services they can use with radio promotions. Most will routinely negotiate rates. If you want to identify your store with a special radio personality, give a tour of your shop to the announcer and let him do an ad from an outline you have provided. Often you get more time than the 30 or 60 seconds allowed for a taped or scripted ad. If your budget is small, you'll get the most from your radio ads if you stagger them by running them two weeks on and one week off. Concentrate airing your ads during a few days of the week or only on the programs listened to by potential customers. Another approach is to air ads only once a year with a blitz on Thursday, Friday and Saturday to announce a special weekend event. Also, if appropriate, explore co-op ads in which you mention the products of your suppliers and share the cost of the radio ads with them.

Television

If you are not careful, you can spend a lot of money on television and get little in return. Television advertising is not a wise choice for most small business retailers. Nevertheless, television commercials are effective if used properly, even by the "little guy." Television advertising cannot be used by the small business owner in the same way that beer companies or auto manufacturers use TV advertising. The small business owner simply doesn't have the budget to air a large number of commercial spots. As a general rule, don't bother with TV ads if you can't purchase enough to repeat your message to your customer base several times a week and maintain the TV ad campaign for three months.

The exception to this rule is placing your commercial advertising on targeted programs. An owner of a local tackle and bait shop does very well by purchasing only one, 30-second commercial each week on a local fishing show. Bargains also can be found on local cable and low frequency stations. The key to success in these cases is to carefully target the programs that will carry your commercial. Most commercial rates are open to negotiation, but remember you must add on the cost to produce the ad, as well as the cost of the air time, to establish your TV advertising budget. Again, look for co-op advertising opportunities.

Some small business owners find it pays to work with a media placement agency to place their TV ads. Since the agencies buy air time in such large quantities, they frequently can negotiate lower rates which they pass on to their clients. In addition, their knowledge of the programming available through local stations can help you get your ads placed on the right programs. TV is a powerful medium and can work wonders; however, it must be used wisely or it can be a very expensive mistake.

Direct Mail

Direct mail advertising can allow a company to carefully target its market. With direct mail marketing, the recipient of the material can be taken right through the entire sales process. By including an order form, coupon or a toll-free number, a company can show what it has to offer and provide a means to make the sale. However, direct mail is very costly and can be ineffective.

Careful planning, testing and a good mailing list are critical to the success of this method. When developing a direct mail piece, gather a collection of direct mail advertising you receive at your home or business. Sort through and save the ones that appeal to you. Then show a few to some of your best customers and ask to which they most likely would respond. Test a few approaches with a limited mailing in advance to see the response rate, then choose the strongest package and send out your mailing. Expect a one to two percent return at most. If you cannot make money with a one or two percent response, don't try direct mail. Also, it often takes two or three repeat mailings to get a prospect to buy.

Direct mail works best for mail order products, but can be used to announce store openings, sales, and new product arrivals.

You can get pre-printed mailing labels from many local and national mailing list companies that can be located in the Yellow Pages. The right mailing list is paramount to success. It is important to get the most up-to-date list for your mailing, so ask the producer when the data for the list was collected and if it is updated on a regular basis. Mailing list companies all charge about the same, but some lists are much better than others.

Some retailers reserve direct mail advertising for prior customers. The response rate is significantly increased when advertising materials are directed at customers already familiar with your store and its goods and services.

What To Send In A Mailing

If you decide to mail to your customers, do so at least twice a year. Many benefits are derived from regular correspondence with your customers, not the least of which is additional sales. Develop a customer mailing piece that includes some of the following suggestions:

Thank customers for their business. Let customers know you appreciate their support and patronage. This gesture promotes good will and strengthens customer loyalty.

Introduce new products. Let your customers be the first to learn about a new product and offer them a special preferred customer discount. This usually will generate an instant increase in sales.

Announce an event. Use a special occasion to communicate with customers about exciting things happening at your store. An anniversary, new location, or an invitation to a preferred customer sale are occasions that give you a reason to contact customers. Offer a special discount, refreshments, a small gift or other incentives to get them to your shop.

Take a survey to uncover customer needs, opinions about your store and complaints about your merchandise or the way you do business. You can put this information to use managing your enterprise and making improvements to your store. Ask customers to rate your services, products, quality, prices, delivery time or return policy on a scale from 1 to 10. Ask for suggestions on improving your business or what new services or products customers would like to see added to your store. Your customers will appreciate the fact that you value their opinions and patronage. Simple, do-it-yourself market research can help you focus on your customer's needs, identify your store's strengths and weaknesses, and help to make sound business decisions.

Solicit testimonials. Ask customers what they like best about what you do or sell. Find out how others react to your merchandise. Ask if your store lives up to their expectations. When you receive favorable responses from your most satisfied customers, ask for permission to quote them in your advertising.

Ask for referrals. Do not overlook this simple method for obtaining new customers. The best form of advertising has always been word-of-mouth. Reward your customers with a small gift or discount if they provide you with the names and mailing addresses of friends that might like to receive your sales information.

Send publicity reprints. When your business or products receive publicity coverage in a local magazine or newspaper, clip the article, make copies and send these to your customers along with other sales materials. This can be done for print ads as well.

Save On Postage

You can cut your postage costs one third by co-oping your mailing. This means finding two other businesses that sell complementary, but non-competing products to a similar customer base and offering to let them "piggy back" their sales literature in your envelope. You can mail four, 8 1/2 inch x 11 inch fliers in a No. 10 envelope for the price of one first-class stamp. Each participating business pays one third of the postage expense plus the cost of a flier. Everyone benefits from such an economical approach. As your business grows and your mailing list numbers more than 200 customers, explore the benefits of obtaining a bulk rate permit to further reduce postage expenses or taking your mailing to a mailing service who can provide bulk mailing rates.

Coupon Co-op Advertising

There are several companies listed in the Yellow Pages under "Advertising Direct Mail" that provide a co-op direct mail service especially effective for coupon advertising to consumers. These companies will design, typeset, print and mail your advertising piece or coupon along with several other non-competing coupon ads to residential homes in the areas of your choice. Each area usually covers approximately ten thousand homes, and clients can have their advertising coupons sent to as many areas as desired. The advertising packs are generally put together and mailed six to eight times a year.

The minimum order usually is one, 2-color coupon or advertising insert to 10,000 homes. Since they are usually targeted to potential customers in the store's service area, the most effective co-op coupons always offer some consumer incentive.

The advantage of this approach is that the cost to mail your material is greatly reduced since it is combined with other advertiser's materials. If this advertising approach has promise for your store, have your coupon art work developed by a professional graphic designer, and ask for an allowance on the rate. Most co-op coupon distributors are simply salespersons. Even though they will claim to be able to design your piece, they have limited knowledge or skill in creating effective coupon ads.

Door Hangers

Announce a sale, special offering, grand opening or event with door hangers. Have your message printed on a heavy paper stock and die cut with a hole to slip on a door handle. Then, hire the local Boy Scout Troop, Little League team or Camp Fire group to distribute them door-to-door in the neighborhoods around your store. Be sure to print a credit line on the door hanger saying ....."This message delivered to you by the Boy Scout Troop #111." You'll get your message delivered with no effort and your donation to the organization for their delivery service will help their fund-raising efforts and establish some "good will" in the community you serve.

Fliers or Circulars

You can use fliers or circulars in hundreds of ways to promote your store. Put them in packages of customers, distribute in parking lots or door-to-door, put on bulletin boards, hand out at trade fairs and shows, mail alone or with other material, hand out on street corners and put in "Take One" racks. Circulars or fliers should tell the reader about special offers and stimulate interest in visiting your store. Raise awareness, provide information and sell your merchandise with a simple flier. If promoting a line of merchandise, make sure you list the benefits and features of the offer and give enough information about where to find it. Fliers also can be given to satisfied customers to pass on to their friends and family. Typeset or produce the flier art work on desk-top publishing and take it to a fast-print shop for production. Creating a half-page flier will allow you to print two on every sheet of paper and stretch your printing dollars without losing much impact.

Postcards

Postcards are an easy and inexpensive way to announce an event, sale, or discount, or to serve as a coupon or reminder notice. Dentists and doctors have used them for years to remind patients about annual or semi-annual checkups. Retail stores might do the same to encourage repeat business. Postcards are easy to use and require less postage than a first-class mailer. Returned, first-class postcards can assist you in maintaining your mailing list and keeping it current. Print hundreds of postcards with your company logo, slogan or symbol on one side and leave the back side blank. Print at least enough to last a year. You can type or hand write messages as needed or take a quantity to a fast-print shop to print a special message or offer on the postcard. Some enterprising business owners print their newspaper or magazine ads on the back of their postcards and mail them to their customers. By so doing, they obtain double duty from their advertising art work.

Take-One Racks

"Take-One" racks are useful for distributing brochures, coupons and product information provided by suppliers. Put them on retail counters to stimulate interest or cross-sell other products and services. Exchange "Take-One" racks with shops offering compatible products or services to the same target market. Make sure you add a "Free" sign on the rack so people will be encouraged to pick up the literature. Add the words "Valuable Coupons" or "Special Offer" and you will sharply increase the distribution of the material in your "Take-One" racks.

Balloons

Use balloons to draw attention to the outside of your retail store or to add a festive touch to a special event. Have the company logo imprinted on the balloon and put clusters of helium filled balloons outside the store. Tie single balloons next to special sale items in the store to draw attention. Balloons also are very successful as give-aways at events that might attract parents and their children. Sales slogans also can be printed on the balloons. Use balloons for customer games and contests. For example, put vouchers good for prizes in selected, air-filled balloons attached to a board or wall and have customers break a balloon to see if they are a prize winner. Release helium-filled balloons with tags advertising your store. Include a balloon with a tag worth a valuable prize for the person finding the lucky balloon.

Billboards

Billboards remind customers of your existence and usually must be accompanied with other forms of advertising to be effective. If you are running a month-long, annual special sale and are using radio and print advertising to announce the event, billboards will work to remind people about the sale. Also, billboards can be effective if you can get the billboard closest to your establishment and put "next exit" or "right at the corner" on the sign. Use a maximum of six or less words and have the billboard designed to make a strong visual statement. One company successfully used a single billboard as the core of its image and positioning strategy. The billboard, located at a highly visible location, was rented by the same firm for years and always carried a dramatic photo of a lion accompanied by a clever slogan. The billboard was consistently a traffic stopper and worked well since the company's name is Lyon Realty. When the billboard was taken down to make way for a commercial development, the event was covered by every major newspaper and TV station in the community. The billboard had become a city landmark. In another case, a giant, round painting of a pizza was attached to a billboard advertising a local pizza parlor. When youngsters stole it as a prank, the "case of the missing pizza" got front page coverage for three days. Sales at the pizza parlor soared. The youngsters were given free pizzas as a reward for returning the billboard section.

Bus Bench/Shelter Signs

This tool is best used with other advertising and serves to remind people of the existence of the business, product or event. Bus bench and bus shelter signs are most effective when placed as close as possible to the business. Because it is not a targeted advertising method, it best serves businesses that have a broad range of customers. Grocery stores, convenience stores, department stores or products like shampoo and toothpaste might consider bus bench signs. A shop on the same block might use a bench or shelter sign as an additional invitation to "Step into Joe's for a Unique Selection of Men's Sportswear," or "You've found Joe's Place; come on in."

Exterior Building Signs

Customers will have difficulty locating a business if adequate signs are not used to identify the company. This is especially true for retail businesses. Not only is a good sign important in helping customers or clients find a business, it can serve as a powerful advertising tool to attract attention from passing motorists and pedestrians. While local building codes or sign ordinances may restrict the size and placement of the store sign, try to have the largest, most visible and highest quality sign you can afford placed in front of your business. Resist using hand-made signs or signs produced with stencils. Your business sign provides one of the first impressions your customer gets and sets the tone for your store's image. Light the sign and you will double its effectiveness. Even if your establishment is closed in the evening, a lighted sign can call attention to the business during nighttime hours.

Point-of-Purchase Signs

These are great for generating cross-selling opportunities or impulse buying. If point-of-purchase advertising signs are not available from the manufacturer or supplier of the products you are selling, make your own. Use a felt tip marker or stick-on letters to create signs that encourage customers to buy. For example, "Just $000," "This model features....," "Ask about our senior's discount," "Free ... with purchase of ...," "On Sale Today," etc. These signs should be placed close to the merchandise to which they are referring. Signs can help close the sale, since people are in the buying mood when they enter the store. Point-of-purchase signs also can be used in promoting special services. Place them in strategic areas to announce payment and credit policies, alterations, gift wrapping and other services you offer.

Video Commercials At Checkout Counters

Store owners with check-out or display counters might consider installing video tape playback machines that will run short commercials on the products and services available in the store. This would be a good vehicle to consider if you are selling new products or if your merchandise is best explained through demonstration. Contact your suppliers and request short videos for use at your store counter. The video tapes can be used to demonstrate, educate, explain, inform and sell. They are especially effective if customers must wait for special services. While they wait, they can learn about your goods and services. A good video tape is like a magnet; it captures the viewer's full attention.

Picket Your Establishment

Pay individuals to picket your establishment with signs that draw attention to your products, special event or sale prices. Use your children and their friends, if necessary. Make sure the signs are large. Use big, dark letters on the signs so passengers in passing cars can read them. This activity can call attention to a sale or new product, especially if the signs are particularly clever. If you call the photo desk of the newspaper in advance of the event, you might land a photo in a local newspaper, as well.

Sidewalk Signs

Place "A" frame signs on the sidewalk or parking lot in front of the store to tell people you are "OPEN" or to announce a "SALE" or special event. Be sure you do not place the signs directly in the way of pedestrians. Chalkboard "A" frame signs are effective for businesses that wish to publicize daily specials. They have worked well for restaurants, bookstores and liquor shops. The purpose of the sidewalk sign is to get the attention of people passing by. Obviously, they work only if the store has a reasonable amount of sidewalk foot traffic. Large "A" frame signs can get the attention of motorists.

Signs Draped on the Building

Large signs or banners can be draped temporarily on a building to announce a "Grand Opening," "Summer Sale," "Now Leasing" or new product line..."Xxx is Here." Hang the fabric signs as close to the top of the building as possible. The higher the sign, the more visible it will be. A sign on a 12-story building will naturally attract more attention than a sign on a 1-story building. Make sure the lettering is large enough to be easily read from a distance. You also can consider hanging banners out the windows or draping a large American flag on the side of a building to get attention.

Window Signs

Put large, simple signs in your window to announce a sale, special offering or special event. This works best when combined with other advertising and promotional activities. However, it is a big mistake to have a permanent "sale" sign in the store window. After a month or two, customers and those passing by will not believe the message and the store will lose credibility. One of the most effective users of simple, paper window signs have been grocery stores. For years, they've put signs advertising their weekly specials in the store windows. The signs work to bring in customers and move merchandise. Hire a local artist to paint holiday designs and greetings on the windows, along with special offers. If window signs are a possibility for you, remember to make them easy to read from a distance and to change them frequently. Visit local fixture and display stores to purchase signs you can place in your windows. These signs carry generic messages and cost much less than custom-made signs.

Personal Sales

Most personal selling efforts will occur on the sales floor of the store. However, some personal sales techniques can be used to influence non-customers and get them to stop by and see what you offer. The following are some methods that take more time than money. Some may prove to be an excellent means for finding new customers.

Business Networking

Join leads clubs, business networking groups, and trade associations to develop business leads and opportunities. You will need to be selective and determine which groups merit your time. Look for organizations with members serving the same target markets as your business or whose members fit your customer profile. Give each organization a 6-to 12-month trial period to assess results. These organizations can provide opportunities to do personal selling, expand your referral base and generate solid business leads. It is a good idea to prepare a brief "30-second commercial" and a 10-minute presentation about your company. If necessary, write your "commercial" on a 3-inch by 5-inch card and carry it with you. Always be prepared to give your "standard pitch" whenever someone asks about your occupation.

Demonstrations

If a picture is worth a 1,000 words, then a demonstration is worth more than a 100 pictures. If you can show your shopper how a product works and how it does exactly what you say it will do, you are more likely to sell it. Because seeing is believing, demonstrations can be your most effective sales presentation. A demonstration allows the viewer to witness the product in action. Prospects see for themselves just how they, too, can achieve the same results from the product.

Through a demonstration, the product sells itself. People will gather around someone who is showing how to use the latest vegetable slicer or exercise equipment, because people just love to see how things work. If your products lend themselves to show and tell, find a place in the store where potential customers can gather for a demonstration.

Door-to-Door Canvassing

Canvassing is the process of seeking out prospective customers and asking for their business. These cold calls are difficult because you only have a few seconds to establish a positive relationship. Try to find something in common with the prospect by talking about something other than the store. Then, give your pitch and ask them to stop by the shop. Always leave a flier or sales sheet with the prospect. Giving free demonstrations or samples when canvassing can help, too. If you have a new store in a neighborhood and provide general consumer products or services, canvass the neighborhood, introduce yourself and invite your new neighbors to the grand opening. Leave fliers or announcements at each stop.

Talks & Presentations

Short talks and presentations before potential customer groups can be an easy way to sell yourself and your products or services. These mini performances give the audience a chance to sample your ability and get to know you personally. They position the speaker as an authority in the field and provide an opportunity to establish credibility and trust. Always give 10-15 minutes of useful information followed by a short question-and-answer period. For example, an apparel store owner might give a talk on how to accessorize an outfit. An electronics store might talk about how to choose equipment. A nursery might give tips on how to plant and maintain flowers, shrubs, trees and grass. Just before you conclude, give a "commercial" about your business. Then, pass around a sign-up sheet requesting names and addresses or business cards from those who might be interested in receiving more information from your company in the future. Put the leads from the business cards and sign-up sheet on your prospect list and follow up with other promotional methods.

Packaging

Put very simply, packaging is the wrapping, box, bag or container that surrounds a product. It serves two purposes - to protect the product and to convey an image. Packaging also can be considered the context in which a service is delivered. For example, a store's environment, including interior design and decoration, serves as the package for the shopping experience.

Depending on the target market, the type of packaging will have varying degrees of importance. Generally speaking, the more upscale the products, the more attention you should pay to the package. Keep this in mind when you select products to feature in your store, packaging for your store's merchandise and your store's overall decoration.

Mailing Labels

If you do mail order sales, make sure your logo and address are printed on all your mailing labels. Better yet, enlarge the labels and make room for your best advertising slogan, as well. This is an easy and effective way to reinforce your marketing messages. Some business owners, who do a high volume of mail order business, change the advertising message on their labels every month.

Package Inserts

Advertise your other products or services by including brochures, fliers, coupons, ad reprints, mail order catalogs and other sales materials in your packages. This works for both retail and mail order companies. Package inserts are great for announcing an upcoming sale, a special promotion or a public relations event. They also can be used to alert customers to a new line of merchandise or services they may not know your store provides. Ask for package inserts from your suppliers. Also, consider exchanging package inserts with a non-competing store that has the same target market. By doing so you can extend your advertising reach with little extra cost or effort. Both businesses can benefit from this kind of promotional arrangement and both stores can save on their advertising costs. Package inserts make good sense. Since you have already sold something to the customer, it is very likely he/she will purchase from you again. Package inserts are an easy way to encourage repeat sales. The main point to remember is to never let a package leave the store without including an advertising insert that encourages the customer to buy from you again.

Stickers

Print stickers with your company logo or name and your telephone number on them. Attach your stickers to products leaving the store. For example, a retail computer store owner attaches his sticker on every computer or printer that leaves the business. He tells customers to call if they have any questions and to use the sticker as a handy reference. The customer always has a visible reminder of the store where the purchase was made and can easily refer another potential customer. Don't skimp on the stickers. Make sure the sticker is attractive. If they look tacky, the customer will simply remove them. Another idea is to place "On Sale" or "20

PERCENT OFF" stickers on merchandise you have marked down. You also can use stickers to add new sales messages to your promotional materials. For example, if you discover another use for a product, announce it with a sticker - "Can be used as..." Finally, colorful stickers make great giveaway items for businesses that sell children's products or services.

Tape or Ribbon

Some clever entrepreneurs have symbols, logos, and sales messages printed on packaging tape or ribbon to remind the customer about where he/she bought the product. This technique is especially useful for stores that sell items in quantity that are stored over a period of time. If the customer makes only occasional purchases, there will be no guessing required to remember what merchant supplied the products - it's on the packaging tape. It's a good idea to print your mailing address and telephone number on the tape, as well. A store name or logo imprinted on the store ribbon used in courtesy gift wrapping will let the recipient know where the gift was purchased.

Gift Wrapping

If appropriate to your merchandise and customer base, you may wish to offer a gift wrapping service. If you are providing a courtesy wrap, be sure your gift box is embossed with your logo, or your store name is printed on a sticker or ribbon to seal the box. A gift wrapping service also can provide additional income and an add-on sale opportunity, especially for the busy customer who doesn't have the time or desire to buy the materials and wrap the gift. Men who are buying gifts appreciate this service and think nothing of paying the added cost for the convience of having the gift wrapped and ready to give when they leave the store.

Public Relations & Publicity

Public relations activities attempt to raise public awareness and gain acceptance and support for a company and its goods and services through means other than paid advertising. Public relations methods include news releases and media relations, sponsorship of special events, charitable benefits, newsletters, thank-you letters, greeting cards and other activities.

Publicity is a public relations function that attempts to raise public awareness through articles and stories in the news media. Though it is difficult to control how the message is conveyed or the vehicle by which it is transmitted, carefully executed publicity programs can be very effective and results often can be achieved at a much lower cost than paid advertising. Today, it is even possible to target the message to potential customers by carefully selecting the media outlets.

Publicity can increase general awareness and help sales, especially in the case of new product launches. Other publicity and public relations activities are aimed at enhancing image and creating awareness and goodwill in a company's community and among a company's potential customers, employees, vendors, regulators and neighbors. Public relations activities generally should be undertaken as part of a company's long-range positioning strategy.

Public relations activities can never be used successfully to cover up bad policy or unethical business practices. Good public relations must start with the business owner's philosophy of doing business. That philosophy flows through the company's policies, procedures and practices. A company's day-to-day business operations often speak clearly for themselves. Public relations deals with reality; not smoke and mirrors.

With that in mind, public relations activities can be used to understand and influence the opinions of groups of people the company depends upon for success. Through these activities, a company can gain support for its position and be seen as a necessary and welcomed part of the community it serves.

For example, some small companies with strong, loyal followings have successfully battled government regulators or local agencies whose decisions might have put them out of business. They took their cases to the court of public opinion through the news media, letter writing campaigns and demonstrations and won reversals of bad decisions. These actions would never have happened if the companies had not cultivated their support groups with good public relations well in advance. Because they were viewed as an asset to the community, others were willing to stand up for them.

For your long-term success, be sure to include some public relations activities in your overall promotion plan. Here are some activities you may wish to consider.

Charitable Events

Charitable giving is as much a part of America as is the free enterprise system. So, participating in the right charitable events can prove to be a "win-win" situation for many businesses and charities. For example, a fashionable, up-scale men's clothing store sponsored a cocktail hour and informal fashion show one Friday evening in the fall. The event was called a "Friday Fall Fashion Fling." Tickets were ten dollars and all proceeds went to a home for runaway youths, of which the store owner was a volunteer member of the governing board. Refreshments were donated and T-shirts commemorating the event were sold. Members of the governing board of the home were all "yuppies" and, of course, they were responsible for selling tickets to the event. Each invited all their yuppie friends who packed the store. All those in attendance had a good time and got more than their money's worth of happy-hour food and drink. The store owner donated a sport coat for a prize drawing. The charity profited and so did the store owner when many in the crowd returned to buy thousands of dollars of clothing. The key to success with these kind of promotional events is to make sure the event, sponsored by the store, will attract potential customers, as well as support a worthwhile charity. With careful planning, everyone comes out a winner.

As another example, a weight control center donated a penny to a local children's hospital for every pound their clients lost during a six month campaign. A picture of huge glass containers filled with pennies being presented to the hospital was printed in the local papers and was a visual testament to the success of the weight control program. The weight control center signed up many new customers following the publicity they received for their charitable donation. Of course, business owners should believe in the charities they are supporting, or customers and friends will soon discover their motives are less than charitable.

Charitable Giving

Direct giving to charitable organizations also can be a powerful tool to create goodwill and acceptance in the community. Charitable giving should be a part of every business budget, even if the budget is modest. Select charities that are personally important to the donor or the employees of a company. If the gift is substantial or significant to the charity, try to acquire some publicity or recognition for the gift so that others will learn of your company's contribution to the community. Small businesses can be very creative in their giving. For example, the employees of one small shop adopted a less fortunate family during the holiday season and provided them with food, clothing, gifts and housewares collected from customers and staff. Their efforts made a nice feature article in the local newspaper and their act of charity brought the employee team closer together. Other companies have donated their products or services or unsold merchandise to non-profit, social service agencies. One manufacturer of children's backyard playground equipment donates a complete set to one local children's program every year. The gift is welcomed and the company is viewed as a generous, civic-minded organization. Team up with your suppliers to look for opportunities to enhance your image by jointly providing donated merchandise to local charities. Giving merchandise to use as door prizes for charity events is another way to gain recognition for your store.

Community Involvement

Another way to make your store visible and develop valuable contacts is to get involved in community development. Joining service organizations, serving on boards of directors for non-profit institutions and encouraging your employees to be active in community activities can help promote your business. In addition, service in these organizations can develop the leadership and organizational skills of your employees - skills that can prove to be useful in the management of the company.

Employee Events

Company picnics, Christmas parties, employee bowling leagues and recreational opportunities can help instill loyalty and pride among employees of a business. When possible and appropriate, it is very helpful to invite the entire employee's family to these events so spouses and children can be better informed about the business. Family members who have enjoyed themselves at the expense of the merchant, often become the store's best promoters.

Grand Openings And Anniversary Celebrations

Plan a grand opening celebration to announce a new business, a new location, or an expansion of existing store. The purpose is to call attention to the business, identify the location and create interest in what the store sells. Grand openings can be simple or elaborate affairs. You may need to support the grand opening with media advertising, a sign on the store, search lights and other activities. Remember, a grand opening event is to attract customers, not entertain family and friends. This is a good time to offer free food and small gifts imprinted with the company logo and location. Promote special merchandise, offer discounts, provide samples, conduct tours and give demonstrations, if appropriate, at the grand opening. The event can be duplicated for significant anniversaries. Such events must be supported by other advertising methods to let people know about the event and to entice them to come.

Greeting Cards

Greeting cards can be an excellent public relations tool. Christmas cards, however, sometimes get lost with all the hoopla of the season and the enormous number of cards that pour in from friends, family and other business owners. Besides, the Christmas shopping season is usually the busiest for most retailers and time to send out Christmas cards doesn't exist. So, you might consider choosing another holiday, perhaps Thanksgiving or the first day of Spring, to send a greeting card to your best customers thanking them for their business and continued support. Birthday or anniversary cards to individual customers are effective for companies providing personal and special services such as hairdressers, florists, jewelers, etc. A jeweler might record the wedding date of all couples buying engagement or wedding rings, being careful to record the new, permanent address of the couple. Then, about three weeks before the first anniversary, the jeweler could send an anniversary card. Of course, it will serve as a reminder to get a gift. The purpose of the cards is to encourage customer loyalty and additional sales. They also serve to remind customers that you are thinking of them on their special day.

Memberships in Organizations

Join the Chamber of Commerce and other business organizations that could be helpful in facilitating your business growth. These organizations are structured to help each business owner or representative make contacts to promote their business. Of course, these organizations are only as good as their leadership and if after a year or so they are not bringing results, you may wish to drop out. Nevertheless, you must be an active member to benefit from any group. Don't simply pay your dues; hang your plaque on the wall and expect things to happen. To gain from membership, a business owner must take time to get involved with activities that will provide opportunities for networking and business relationships to develop naturally. Membership in business organizations is especially useful for the merchant who depends on referrals. The contacts made through these organizations can be vital if a business owner ever needs to rally support for a cause from other business associates.

Personalities

Sometimes associating your store with a personality or celebrity can increase sales. Because most small business owners cannot afford a nationally known figure to make an appearance, they may find suitable personalities in the community. A radio announcer, college coach, TV weatherman, local athlete, politician, or a beauty queen may be just what your business could use to gain attention. You can pay them to appear at a special event, such as a grand opening, major sale, charity event, etc. When you make it possible for people to meet a celebrity in person, they often respond by becoming loyal customers. If you decide to use a personality at an event, remember the purpose is to increase foot traffic and sales, so think of every possible angle to announce the appearance of the personality in advance to draw a crowd of potential customers.

Special Events

Special events can be staged to generate excitement and publicity for almost any store, or business for that matter. Here are four examples. Every year in the spring, a local restaurant called the Marble Club holds an annual marble shooting contest with the proceeds going to charity. The staff of one hospital challenged another to a hospital bed pushing race down the city's main street. A landscaping company built a large sand castle on its grounds. A bicycle shop held a bike repair clinic. Special events can include open houses, tours, late-night sales and holiday activities. When planning a special event, be sure to notify the news media and try to obtain some publicity. Remember, special events should be designed to increase awareness and attract new customers, as well as generate some excitement and interest in the event. Be sure to plan a special event well in advance and try to anticipate all the details that must be executed to make the event a success. Always advertise and promote the event in order to get participation; otherwise, you may throw the party and have nobody attend.

Sponsorships

Carefully selected business sponsorships can create attention, help establish credibility in the community and reach a target market at a reasonable cost. Sponsorships can even produce sales if, for example, your sponsorship of an event is tied into having the organizers purchase and sell your merchandise at the event. By visibly supporting your target market's favorite activities or charities you enhance the image of your store while reinforcing your message through life-style identification. Some sponsorships also can provide an entertainment event for you to host your preferred customers and an opportunity to sample, display or demonstrate your merchandise. Sponsorship of a Little League team, bowling team, tennis tournament, charitable event, turtle race, or a marble shoot can create attention and raise public awareness about your business. However, unless carefully designed to do so, don't expect these sponsorships to produce immediate sales. Sponsorships do provide goodwill, raise awareness and help to solidify the loyalty of existing customers. That is why established businesses more frequently use sponsorships as part of their overall public relations effort. If you choose to do sponsorships, make sure they relate in some way to your business and look to the long term for results.

Thank You Notes

Always find a way to thank your customers. Send a thank you note or postcard to all customers who make major purchases. Personalize the thank you as much as possible and indicate how pleased you would be if the recent customer would make referrals to your company. This tool is simple, easy and effective. Yet, it is surprising how many business owners never take the time to show appreciation to their customers and clients. Also, be sure to thank referral sources for sending you business. A major bank lost a valuable customer who had referred thousands upon thousands of dollars of business to the bank, as well as personally controlled several accounts with huge deposits. The banker never bothered to acknowledge the source of the referrals, let alone send a verbal or written thank you. As a result, the referral source felt unappreciated and moved his business and his referrals elsewhere. His comment tells the whole story when he said, "I guess you just have to move your business around to keep from being taken for granted."

Seek Free Publicity

What is publicity? Publicity is free advertising disguised as a news story. A feature article in the daily newspaper about you and your business can generate extraordinary interest in what you do and what you sell. Exposure through the news media can really boost sales, as well as establish business credibility.

Publicity has two big advantages over advertising. First, publicity is more credible to the public, because it is perceived as news, something of interest or something important. Second, the business does not pay for the print space or broadcast airtime. Obtaining publicity, however, takes time and effort. Contacting reporters about your business and enticing them to write a story can be time consuming and sometimes frustrating.

To get your business in the news, you must develop an "angle;" a unique slant to your story that offers the media something special or different to report. Your "angle" must be newsworthy, provide human interest or tie into a current trend or topic. For example, the co-author, Susan Ratliff, obtained four feature articles with photos about her business in Arizona newspapers when she mentioned to reporters that she was a career woman turned entrepreneur after the birth of her son. This topic, the woman on the career track switching to the mommy track, then to the entrepreneur track, was her angle. It was a timely topic of interest for many readers of the newspapers that published the articles and the journalists were happy to report it.

Barbara Lambesis was able to build her credibility and business as a marketing consultant by being featured in Inc. Magazine and other national business publications. Her "angle" was her motive for starting a business. As a corporate executive who hit the glass ceiling, she represented thousands of other women who dropped out of the corporate sector to start their own business.

Your angle might be anything unusual such as a store owned and operated by twins or triplets, a store with all handicapped employees, or a store with unusual merchandise or service. Look for something within your business to use as your "angle."

Newsworthy topics also include receiving an award, holding a contest, sponsoring an event, introducing a new product, writing a book, teaching a seminar or expanding the company. The information you give the media must educate, enlighten, amuse or inform the general public. It also must be timely. Always send publicity information to the media at least two weeks in advance of an event to meet deadlines for weekly publications. The newspapers cannot help publicize your event if you don't supply the information prior to their deadlines.

Once you decide on an angle for your story, plan your approach for contacting the media. Contact the small, community papers first. You can make a few mistakes learning the ropes with these publications without ruining your chances for placing a story.

Start by placing a phone call. If you have a business angle, call the newspaper and ask to speak to the business editor. If your angle is of general interest to the readers, ask for the features editor. Tell the editor you would like to discuss a story idea. Explain your story, using your "angle" to interest the editor in assigning a reporter. Be sure not to pitch your product or services directly. When a pitch is too commercial, the editor will take offense and tell you to contact the advertising department about buying ad space. If your idea is appealing, editors will request additional information in writing or schedule an interview immediately.

News Releases

When the media requests written information about a story idea, the standard format used to respond is a news release. Send a brief, one-page, double-spaced information sheet to the news media to announce new products, a new location, business milestones or appointments of new key personnel. Also use news releases to attempt to get general publicity about your company. Try to seize every opportunity to keep your name in front of the public through the news media. The news media, especially your local newspapers and magazines, can help create familiarity and credibility for your business. Also appear on radio and TV talk shows, if appropriate, and give useful information to the consumer. Working with the media can enhance the credibility of business owners and help establish them as the local experts in their fields. A news release is the best method to approach the media with newsworthy information, but don't rule out a quick telephone call to a reporter or the news desk with an item that might get their attention.

Each release competes with hundreds of other releases, so it must be both intriguing and concise in order to gain attention. A well-written news release should begin with an attention-grabbing headline, followed by a paragraph that answers the questions who, what, when, where, why and how, as it pertains to your product, service, event or store. Examine every detail about your business to determine what you might have to offer the media.

WHO? Who are you in the community? Who benefits from your products or services? Who do you know that might have an impact on your appeal to the media? Who should attend the event you are planning?

WHAT? What do you do? What is your product or service? What event are you involved with? What can you teach someone? What have you achieved or invented? What difficulties have you faced? What have you overcome to get where you are?

WHEN? When did you get started? When will your products be available? When should the information be released? When does the offer expire? When does the event take place?

WHERE? Where can your products be found? Where are you from? Where were you educated? Where did you learn what you do? Where do your products come from?

WHY? Why should anyone be interested in what you do or sell? Why did you pursue this business venture? Why does anyone need what you have? Why do you want the public to know this information?

HOW? How did you get started? How can someone benefit from your offerings? How can someone get what you're offering? How does it work? How good is it? How do you make it?

Use the standard format when composing your news release. Type, double spaced, all the information on one side of an 8 1/2 inch by 11 inch sheet of paper. Include the words FOR IMMEDIATE RELEASE in the top left corner, skip down three spaces then put CONTACT: followed by your name, address and phone number. Skip down a few spaces then type your headline followed by a paragraph that answers who, what, when where, why and how. Reporters are under strict space and time constraints, so express your ideas and information plainly, concisely and in as short a space as possible. Present the information in descending order of importance. If the editor must review hundreds of releases, you must present the most important and compelling information in the first paragraphs, since the last half of a release may never be read. Information in the first paragraph should sum up the complete idea of the story angle.

After sending the information to the reporter, wait a week, and follow up with a phone call. Inquire whether the information was received and if there are any questions concerning the facts. You'll get an indication from the conversation whether the reporter is interested in pursuing the story further. Don't hesitate to ask if there is an interest in the idea. If turned down, approach again in a few months with a slightly different angle.

Publicity can have a beneficial impact on your business. The time and trouble it takes to cultivate publicity is well worth the effort. If you feel unable to handle this task by yourself, hire a professional public relations firm to help you.

Sales Incentives

Sales incentives are methods used to get prospective customers to buy your merchandise. Sales incentives of one kind or another have been used effectively by most retailers. Some companies depend on them heavily to promote their business. For most businesses, sales incentives should be only a part of a total promotion plan. In addition, they should be carefully selected and planned so they reach and motivate primarily new, preferred customers.

Unfortunately, many sales incentive programs are wasted on loyal customers who are already willing to pay full price for the merchandise and who do not require an incentive to purchase again. Of all the methods available to promote a business, sales incentive methods can be the most risky and the most costly.

Sales incentives remain attractive because they can have a dramatic, instant effect on sales. They are designed to entice the potential customer to try an offering for the first time or buy more than planned. Before you jump on the sales incentive bandwagon, remember marketing experts have long agreed that all good incentives must do four things to be successful.

First, they should support and enhance the image of the business. The sales incentive should be appropriate for the business and should be able to help improve the store's position in the market place.

Second, they should inspire the user to purchase products at the store again. Just getting a customer to buy once is not enough. Incentives should be designed to encourage repeat sales.

Third, they should be aimed at prospects and should motivate them to buy. Many sales incentive programs fail because they do not reach or motivate potential *new* customers.

Finally, they should create some sense of urgency. Prospects should feel that if they don't act now, they will lose an important opportunity.

Sales incentives have some real pitfalls that must be considered before a retailer decides to include them in the company's promotion plan. Unfortunately, all sales incentives only provide short-term gains. Stop the incentives, and you usually stop the sales. Incentives can give an immediate boost to the bottom line, but usually will not sustain growth once the incentive is withdrawn. In addition, people who are enticed by sales incentives are not inclined to become loyal customers.

Unfortunately, if enticed to buy through a sales incentive, most of these customers often will not return to buy at the regular price. They will require another sales incentive to purchase again. Finally, all sales incentives have a big impact on profit - they reduce it. All sales incentives have a direct or indirect price cutting or profit eroding effect. Therefore, a sales incentive program must make up in volume what it will lose in profit margins. Nevertheless, in most highly competitive businesses, it is not possible to completely avoid sales incentive programs and still survive. The following are some sales incentive promotions to consider:

Contests

Contests and games can attract customers and appeal to everyone's desire to be the lucky winner. You should be careful to check with your lawyer to be sure a proposed contest or sweepstakes is legal in your area. Cash is the most attractive prize, but other items will do nicely. You might consider offering your products as the prize. One art supply store held a children's coloring contest by offering free, blank posters at the check-out counter. Parents made additional purchases of crayons, magic markers and colored pencils to give their children a better chance to win. To enter, the completed poster had to be returned to the store. This created another buying opportunity. The prize? Art supplies, naturally. And, since the promotional expenses were shared by three stores in the chain, the cost was minuscule. Offering your merchandise as a prize can help you develop a mailing list of prospects interested in your offerings from those participating in the contest. Also, you may wish to offer a consolation prize to contestants who do not win. A small, inexpensive item can be offered if the contest loser is willing to come to your place of business to pick it up. Once in the store, the loser may be enticed to buy your goods and services. Remember, games and contests should be fun and exciting. The more you can involve the customer in the contest, the better.

Discount Coupons

The discount coupon is a commonplace and popular method to get people to try products or services for the first time. They can be attached to the product for immediate redemption, handed out with canvassing, stuffed in packages, given with free samples, mailed separately or with other material. You may wish to distribute special coupons to separate target market groups. Coupons can be distributed in hundreds of ways, so print thousands. Hand out coupons at trade fairs, swap coupons with another company to use as package stuffers, pin coupons on community bulletin boards, put them on car windshields in parking lots, or send them along with your billings. Be sure to put the name and location of your company or store on the coupon, as well as information about the product and discount. Put a time limit on the coupon to create a sense of urgency. Studies show that only about 3 percent of the coupons distributed are ever redeemed. Moreover, a coupon must offer at least a 20 percent discount to be effective. Try to put your coupons in the hands of non-customers. Unfortunately, about 60 percent of the coupons redeemed are done so by loyal consumers who would have gladly paid full price. Therefore, be sure to target your coupons to prospects, not existing customers.

Discount Premium Books

Consider placing an ad in local discount premium books. They generally contain coupons making two-for-one offers or discounts that are redeemed at the business. You can easily test to see how much new business was brought in through this method by simply saving the coupons and checking the results. Have customers who redeem the coupons write their name and address on the back. Use the information to develop a mailing list and send them advertising and sales information. Just because customers tried your establishment once by using the premium book coupon doesn't mean they will remember to visit your business again. It takes several visits to get a customer into the habit of selecting your store and thinking of you first.

Free Trials

If your products lend themselves to a "free" trial offer, consider this incentive for your potential customers. Free trial offers should not be limited to test driving cars or a visit to the health spa. Some appliance, furniture and exercise equipment stores offer a 30-day, free home trial period for qualified customers. The whole idea behind free trial offers is simple. If you try it, you will like it, and if you like it, you will buy it.

Free trial offers are especially suited for items that do not attain immediate customer acceptance or items and services that people are reluctant to purchase for fear they will not like it once they have bought it. Once a product gets in the home, rarely is it returned within the time limit.

Gifts And Premiums

For businesses with big ticket items or services, offering a free gift or premium with the purchase can be an incentive to get the customer to buy. Try to tie-in the promotion with another company to stretch the effectiveness of the incentive and lower the cost of the gifts and premiums. Even merchants with smaller ticket items or services might consider this approach. Offer an item free or at a greatly reduced cost with a minimum purchase of your products. "Buy $50 or more of any of our gift items and receive a free set of four holiday goblets." "Open your charge account with us and receive a free pocket calculator." If you decide to use gifts or premiums, make sure the items you choose are attractive to and appropriate for your potential customers. A good example is a pet store that once offered a dog obedience training book free with the purchase of a 50-pound sack of dog food and a dog leash.

Multiple Purchase Offers

When you offer a customer "one free" after they have purchased a certain number of items, you are making a multiple purchase offer. Donut shops, hair cutting salons, ice cream parlors and car washes have used this method successfully to get customers to keep coming back. Once a customer has made five or ten purchases, the next one is free. To keep track of the purchases, issue each customer a small card they can keep in their wallet and punch a hole in the card with each purchase. Or, you can keep the customer cards on file at your business and record the purchases yourself. This is the best way, since you can get the name and mailing address of your customers without effort and use the cards to develop a mailing list. Multiple purchase offers usually get the customer back several times. Rarely, however, do most customers complete the number of purchases required to get the "one free."

Price Specials

Family rates, student and senior discounts, and group discounts are just some of the ways you can offer price incentives to attract a certain segment of the market. Don't use this tactic on groups that are already willing to pay full price. This incentive should be offered to new markets you wish to attract. Seniors are especially attracted to businesses who offer special treatment for senior citizens. Since they usually have lots of time, seniors are more willing to go out of their way to do business at an establishment that is perceived to give them a special price.

Rebates

Offering a cash rebate for a purchase of a product can stimulate sales. If the purchaser must complete a form and provide proof of purchase to obtain the rebate, it is surprising how many won't bother. This is often the case, even when the offer of the rebate was the incentive to make the purchase in the first place. Small ticket items can offer rebates of $1 - $5, and be just as successful in moving goods as the car manufacturer who offers rebates of $500 or more. The consumer finds rebates less desirable than other price incentives because he has to work harder to get the savings. Check with your vendors to determine if rebates can or should be offered to move inventory.

Referral Incentives

Offer an incentive for referrals. Gifts, prizes and merchandise can be offered as an incentive to get current customers and associates to refer business to your store. Regardless of how large or small the referral incentive is, always be sure to thank the referral source. The "thank you" is often more important to the referring party than the reward. Some businesses announce the referral programs up front to the potential referral sources and encourage them to participate. Others find it more tasteful to simply acknowledge a referral with a flower arrangement, gift certificate to a restaurant or small gift from the shop immediately after the unsolicited referral has been made. One idea is to ask your current customers to bring a friend in during customer appreciation week. If both make purchases during the shopping trip, each receives a 5 percent discount. All referral incentives should be in keeping with industry practices and the company image. Referral incentives can be very effective when it comes to getting other people to send you customers.

Sampling

Customers flock to stores that give free samples. Sampling, as a method to entice sales, has worked successfully for retailers with products such as cookies, cinnamon rolls, salsa, pickles, coffee, tea, make-up, perfumes, flowers or stationery. If you decide to use this method to attract customers, be sure to consider whether the benefits of sampling outweigh the costs. Always provide printed material and ordering information with each sample.

When appropriate, hire someone in an unusual costume to draw attention to the giveaway item. Hand out samples on a busy street corner or near public entrances to your store. If practical, place the sample in a plastic bag and deliver door-to-door, hanging samples on door knobs. Samples can be mailed or included with another product or service. Be sure to give information about where to obtain the product at the time of sampling. It also is a good time to hand out a discount coupon as an additional incentive to get the potential consumer to buy the product after he has tried the sample. Work with your vendors to set up a sampling program if you think it will work for your store.

Special Sales

Don't just have a sale, have a happening. Some stores have "midnight madness sales" and open their doors at midnight to clear out old inventory or special purchases. One store had a "crack of dawn sale" and offered free breakfast in the parking lot for everyone who made a purchase of $25 or more between the hours of 5 and 8 a.m. A "sidewalk sale" also is an old standby. The idea is to do something so unusual that your company will be remembered for its special sale event.

Tie-ins With Other Businesses

Identify complementary businesses that serve the same target market as your retail store. Look for inventive ways to jointly promote your businesses. For example, offer your merchandise or service as a prize to a radio or TV show for use in return for a negotiated number of mentions about your store. Have your fliers distributed in another company's packaging. A pizza parlor chain offered free soft drinks with a purchase, while the soft drink company attached pizza coupons to its product. Have your announcements or fliers inserted in the billing statements of other companies in exchange for including their information in your packages. Both companies will benefit from these arrangements.

Two-for-One Offers

Offering two-for-the-price-of-one can be an effective method to get two people to try your product for the first time. Twofers, as they are called by marketing professionals, work well for events charging admission, but also have been successful promoting goods and services. Limit the offering to a short time period to create some urgency. Two-for-one offers are better than offering 50 percent off because they either move two items with each purchase or introduce two customers to the product or service.

Get Organized

Now that you have discovered many ideas for promoting your store, go back through this chapter and review the activities you think will work for your establishment. Think again about your target market and your prospective customers. Carefully consider whether or not the methods you are considering will be effective ways to reach and motivate your prospects.

Next, determine if your budget can afford to implement the activities you have selected. Remember, you must repeat the activity several times to get the prospective customer's attention. So, determine if your budget can afford to repeat the method often enough during the next year to be effective. Then, select the best 10-12 methods you think will work for your business and list them on the work sheet at the end of this chapter. Review the sample promotion plan for The Flower Warehouse, also at the end of this chapter, to give you a better idea of how to organize and balance a simple plan for your retail store.

Key Sales Messages

Next, list the advantages of your offering and the reasons why your goods or services should appeal to potential customers. List the benefits, both practical and psychological, that your store offers. Your messages may have to do with convenience, price, quality, or friendly service. To get consumer attention, use words and phrases like "save," "brand new," "results proven," "easy," "free," "effective," "now," "guarantee" and "sale" in your key sales messages. These messages should be incorporated into all your promotional activities, including advertising, packaging, personal sales, public relations/publicity and sales incentives.

Develop A Sales Slogan

In ten words or less, describe your company's greatest asset in the eyes of your customers. Use this as your sales slogan.

Now, consider if your sales slogan and key sales messages can be effectively delivered through the promotion methods you are considering. Make any necessary adjustments to the activities you selected. Determine the frequency of use and the annual estimated cost of each activity. Add any helpful comments in the space provided on the work sheet. When you are finished, you will have an easy-to-follow promotion plan for your business. Review the plan each month to determine what specific activities you should be implementing. Again, the example plan for a flower shop at the end of this chapter should provide a better idea of what your promotion plan should look like.

Stick To Your Plan

If you fail to let potential customers or clients know about the benefits they will receive from your goods or services, or if you do little or nothing to promote your business, it is unlikely your business will be able to survive or prosper. Promoting your business stimulates sales, and sales make your business a success.

You will feel more comfortable promoting your business with a simple, carefully crafted plan of action in which you select 10-12 promotional activities that will reach and motivate your potential customers. Use information you gather from your current customer base to help you determine the best methods. Talking to your customers is the easiest and most affordable means of doing market research. Your customers will probably come up with your sales slogan if you simply ask them what they like best about your store. In addition, they can tell you about how they learned about your business in the first place and which promotional methods they respond to most frequently. Once you have selected the appropriate activities, you must make a strong commitment to your plan and implement it on a consistent basis.

Your plan will fail if you do not set aside time, energy and money to put the plan into action. Make sure that the messages you deliver to your prospects will motivate them to buy from you. The messages you send are as important to the success of your promotion plan as the methods you use as vehicles to send them. Again, rely on your current customers to help you select the most effective messages. Understand what your customers need and want from you and stress how your business can satisfy those needs better than your competitors. From your customer's point of view, describe your greatest business asset or the most appealing aspect of your business in ten words or less and turn it into your sales slogan. Remember, repeat your sales slogan in all your advertising and promotional activities.

Give It Time To Work

Stick to your plan. Don't panic if you don't get instant results. Few promotional plans that are implemented on a small budget ever become an overnight success. You must be willing to give your plan time to work. Again, you can increase the effectiveness of your promotional activities by consistently repeating them as often as your budget can afford. It is better to do a few things well and repeat them over and over, than it is to do many things once or once in a while. Evaluate the effectiveness of each of your promotional activities only after you have given each one enough time to fairly judge the results.

Try to have fun promoting your business. That will help get rid of some of the anxiety business owners often feel about marketing, advertising and promotion, and about spending money on these activities. Most retailers would love to just open the doors and ring up sales at the cash register without having to make an effort to attract customers. Unfortunately, that rarely happens. So, if your business survival must depend on promoting your store, you might as well try and have some fun doing it.

Many promotional activities allow the business owner to personally get to know their customers. Often they discover they really enjoy the company of their customers and have things in common with them other than the business relationship. Friendships develop. Some promotional activities also offer an opportunity to entertain clients, support interests outside the business or make a contribution to the community. When this happens, you should view the activity not only as an investment in the company's promotion plan, but also as one of the side benefits of business ownership.

We wish we could give credit to the marketing genius who came up with the saying "people just love to buy from people who love to sell." That person was right on the money with his observation. There is nothing as effective as enthusiasm when it comes to promoting your business, selling your merchandise or convincing another business owner to do a joint promotion. Enthusiasm is contagious; it's also a powerful tool of persuasion. So, be enthusiastic about your business and about promoting it every chance you get.

Finally, of all the activities a business owner must undertake to develop and manage a successful business, promotional activities - advertising, packaging, personal sales, public relations/publicity and sales incentives - conducted on behalf of the company have the most impact when it comes to telling the world about what kind of store the owner operates. A company's promotional activities are the windows through which an outsider first sees into a business and often they determine whether or not the outsider will open the door and step in.

Promotion Plan Flower Warehouse

Promotional Method	Frequency	Annual Cost	Comments
Yellow Pages	Daily	$2,400	Monitor Results
Window Signs	12 x Year	$360	Support Promotions
Point of Purchase Signs	12 x Year	$240	Support Promotions
Newspaper Ads	2 x Month	$3,000	Support Promotions
Fliers	12 x Year	$800	With Sales Promotions
Sales Promotions	1 x Month	$4,500	Holidays & Specials
Publicize Publicity	12 x Year	$200	Promotions
Personal Sales Calls	1 x Week	$0	Corporate Accounts
Sampling & Gifts	as needed	$1,000	Door Prizes Referrals
Networking	1 x Week	$600	Sales Leads
Thank You Letters	as needed	$0	Customers Referrals

Promotion Plan - YourCompany

Promotional Method	Frequency	Annual Cost	Comments

CHAPTER EIGHT

Changing Direction

There are three critical turning points store owners may face that could force them to change directions. The first is before the store ever exists and market research indicates the proposed retailing concept is not financially viable in the territory the business owner is considering. At this point, it is foolish for a business person to continue developing a store in view of the findings. To do so courts disaster and usually results in owners losing their money and their pride.

Unfortunately, many retailers are so convinced their concept will succeed and are so emotionally attached to it they forego the simple market research necessary to make a sound business decision. Follow your instincts, but use your brain. Be disciplined enough to undertake the steps necessary to determine if your concept will fly before you invest all your money, time, energy and ego into a retail store. If the project is not feasible, be thankful you had a chance to pull out before you committed yourself to a losing cause.

The second turning point usually comes after the store has been open six to nine months and things are not going as planned. This usually is the case for retailers who did not do their homework initially, but also happens occasionally to store owners whose market research and business plan gave them a strong indication they could succeed. Change will be necessary to salvage the store or it soon will be out of business.

The third turning point comes when stores that have a history of success find their sales slowly declining over a couple of years. Rather than hang on to an old retail concept, they may need to change direction or update their approach to regain lost customers and find new ones in the same sales territory.

When Things Are Not Working

The decision to make changes is not an easy one, especially for store owners who have enjoyed success and feel comfortable doing things the way they have been done for years. Here are some early signals to look for that indicate change may be necessary.

* A decline in foot traffic or an inability to attract a reasonable share of the foot traffic in the area.

* Difficulty in reaching sales goals for three consecutive months.

* Inability to motivate shoppers to buy, even with sound promotional and advertising activities.

If store owners have employed many of the ideas found in this book and have aggressively marketed and promoted their business but sales are still too slow to make a go of the enterprise, it's time to change direction.

Remember, customers are fickle. Trends and fads come and go. Moreover, long-term customer loyalty is almost non-existent. Therefore, retailers must be ready to adapt or change in order to meet the changing needs and wants of customers.

Assessing The Market

In order to find out why your retailing concept is not working, you must take time to assess the market. Carefully examine the market territory of your store. Most urban and suburban independent stores must draw their customers from a radius of one and a half miles from the store. Those stores in large or regional malls and shopping centers will draw customers from approximately five miles from the location.

Demographics

Check the demographics of your territory and compare them to previous years. Are your type of customers moving in or out of your territory? Are the residents of your territory a stable or changing population? If your territory has a stable population, are the residents aging in such a way that you should acquire or lose more customers in the age group that most often buys from your store. Remember, retailing and selling is a numbers game. There must be sufficient numbers of your potential customers in your market territory to make your concept work. Shoppers are looking for convenience. So, unless your store is truly unique and extraordinary, shoppers will not travel long distances to buy what you have to offer. You must depend on drawing your customers from your surrounding area.

Competition

Has new competition moved into your territory? If so, what has been the impact and what have you done to counter the attack? Look for direct and indirect competitors. A direct competitor offers similar products and services to the same customer type. An indirect competitor offers products and services that are not similar, but could be substituted for those you offer. For example, a candy store and yogurt shop are indirect competitors. While the products are not the same, both are trying to sell to the customer with a craving for sweets and are indirectly competing for the same customer's dollar. Indirect competition also occurs when two stores in the same territory offer the same products but to different customer types. For example, a women's clothing store that offers petite sizes is an indirect competitor of a women's clothing store in the same territory that offers large sizes.

Usually an increase in competition will mean the store owner must step up promotional activity to keep existing customers and capture new ones. Shop the competition to see what they are offering to customers by way of merchandise, price, atmosphere and customer service. Then, match or better what they are doing. Feed off their promotion and position your store as the best in the territory for the combination of convenience, friendliness, quality and price.

If you discover there are far too many competitors chasing far too few potential customers, then your options for change must go beyond simply stepping up your marketing and merchandising effort.

Social, Political And Economic Trends

Social, political and economic trends influence greatly what consumers will purchase in the marketplace. Keep your hand on the pulse of these trends to be one step ahead of changing consumer buying habits. In the 1980s when glamor, glitz and greed were in, high ticket luxury items and conspicuous spending on non-essential items were in fashion.

By the early 1990s, that trend had died and consumers concentrated their spending on practical goods and products they thought would provide comfort and security.

Take, for example, what Mercedes Benz did to adjust to changes in the marketplace. In the 80s, its selling approach was to appeal to consumer's, primarily yuppies, desire for status and luxury. By purchasing and driving a Mercedes, the owner could show the world he/she had arrived, was successful and could afford a luxury automobile. In the 90s, the company used a different selling approach to sell the same product. The appeal was to families and their desire to protect their children. Mercedes was being positioned as the safest car on the road, and worth the investment required to protect one's family in case of an accident.

By anticipating these trends, you can change your merchandise mix and promotional thrust to be in sync with current consumer beliefs and attitudes.

Looking At Options

There are several options available to the store owner who must make radical changes. If the profitability of the store is no longer viable, what can a business owner do?

Close The Store - A painful as this might be, it's better to cut your losses as early as possible once you are convinced the existing store concept will not make it at its current location.

Move To A New Location - If you have indications that your concept is appealing, but you simply do not have enough of your customer type in your territory to be profitable, move the store to a new location. Be sure your concept is viable, however. Get sufficient feedback from your existing customers and conduct adequate market research when selecting a new location.

Change The Concept - If you are determined to stay at the same location, are willing to do some market research and are open to considerable change, then you should consider adopting a new retail concept at your current location. For example, a look at current and projected demographics might tell you to change your dress shop from one aimed at mature women to one aimed at juniors 16-25 years of age. Or, to change your merchandise from high-end items to discount products. In all cases, you will probably be required to remodel the store, change it's name and launch the new concept with an aggressive promotional effort to distinguish the old store from the new one.

Make A Business Decision

Most business owners are emotionally attached to their companies. Retailers are no different. That's what makes change difficult and tough decisions hard to make. When forced to make decisions about the future of your store, be sure to involve some advisors that can help you assess the situation objectively. A banker, accountant, lawyer or business consultant often can wade through the emotional considerations and help an owner make a more pragmatic decision. A store, after all, is suppose to be a money making business. Once it stops making money or fails to achieve profitability, an owner is forced to cut his losses and move on or make the drastic and sometimes uncomfortable changes necessary to turn the store around.

To make money retailing, an owner must be willing to make the constant changes necessary to improve the merchandising concept and bring value and pleasure to each customer's shopping experience. If you are willing to make such changes, you will see the rewards of your efforts by making more money from your retail store.